30DAY SEX
CHALLENGE
A JOURNEY TO INTIMACY

30DAYSEXCHALLENGE – A JOURNEY TO INTIMACY

©2008 Paulwirth.org.

All Scripture quotations unless otherwise indicated are taken from The Holy Bible, New Living Translation (NLT), Copyright © 1996. Used by permission of Tyndale House Publishers, Inc., Wheaton, Illinois 60189.

Other Scripture references are taken from the following sources: The Message (MSG), copyright © 1993. Used by permission by NavPress Publishing Group.

New American Standard Bible (NASB), copyright © 1960, 1977, 1995 by the Lockman Foundation.

The Holy Bible, New International Version (NIV). Copyright © 1973, 1978, 1984, International Bible Society. Used by permission of Zondervan Bible Publishers.

Scripture quotation identified as KJV is from the King James Version of the Bible.

Cover Design and Layout by Leslee Workman – inspired2serve.com

Special Thanks to Martha Fry

Back Cover photo by: 12-1photography.com

We dedicate this work first to our loving family,

Thanks for your love, prayers, and support!
To Ashlyn and Anthony, you know that Mommy and Daddy love each

other very much! We are so full of joy over

you two precious gifts from God!

& to our family at Relevant Church,
May we all lead by example in our marriages!

TABLE OF CONTENTS

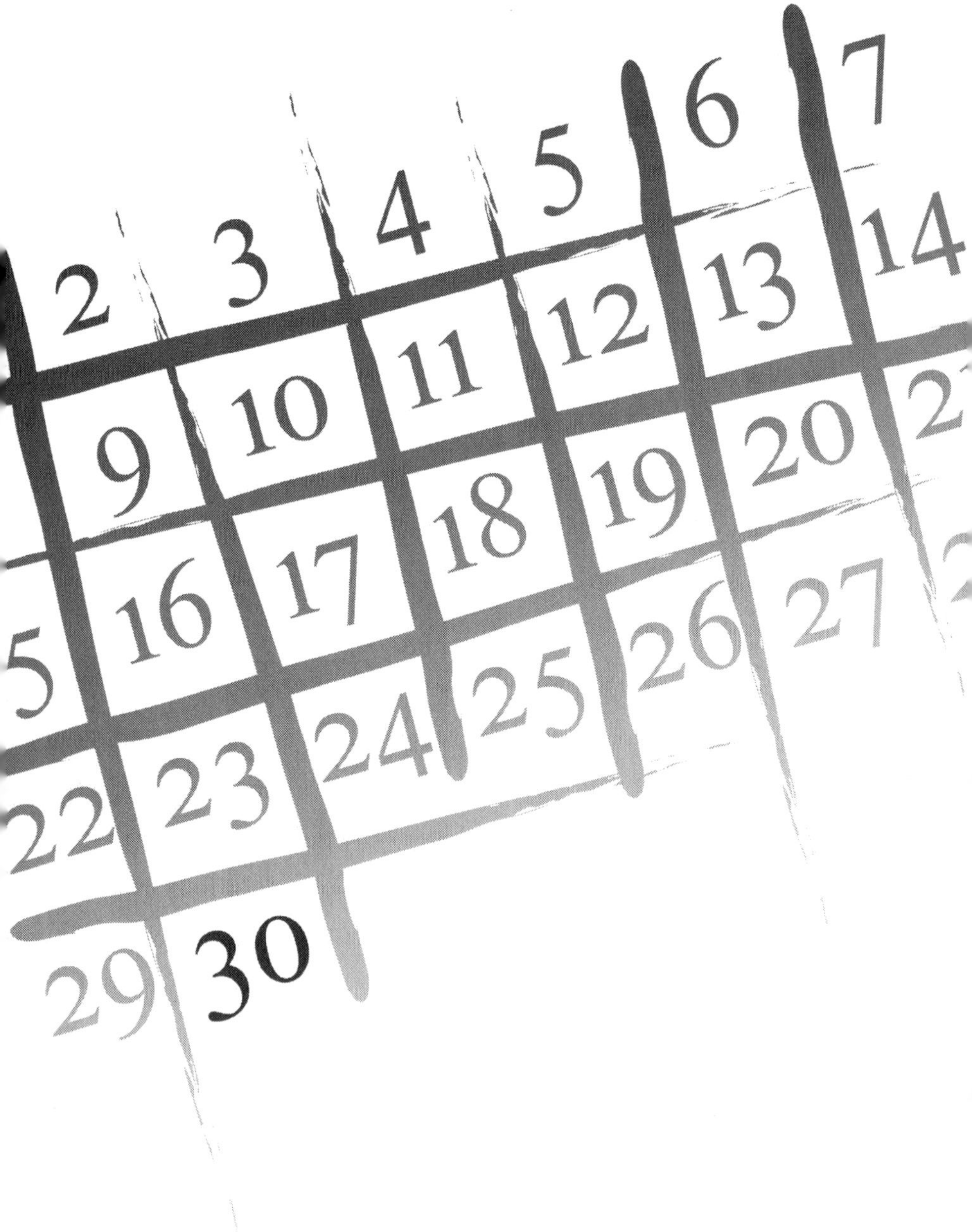
2 3 4 5 6 7
9 10 11 12 13 14
16 17 18 19 20
22 23 24 25 26 27
29 30

PREFACE

30daysexchallenge-A Journey to Intimacy is a workbook designed to lead couples on a journey of marital fulfillment.

We are not psychologists, therapists, or licensed counselors. We are a Pastor and his wife who have worked in full or part-time ministry for over 16 years. We have been married for over 18 years. We are unashamedly Followers of Jesus Christ.

That said this book is not intended to be a religious book. It is, however, based on divine guidance and is written from a Christian worldview. Our opinions are based on Biblical principles and tenants. Our advice is based on what God has revealed to us through Scripture as He has worked on our lives and on our marriage.

We have been asked if this book can be useful to couples who do not believe in the Bible. Our answer is emphatically "yes"!

However, we believe that God created us and is, therefore, the ultimate authority on our lives and relationships. We derive His instruction from His Word, the Bible. It would be impossible for us to write this book without referencing the words that have enlightened us.

Our hope is that those who do believe in God and His Son, Jesus Christ, will gain a greater understanding of His plan for your lives – a plan that we believe involves an on-going cycle of forgiveness and reconciliation.

And for those non-believers that will read the book, we are not ignorant of the fact that the idea of 30 days of sex which is the ultimate goal of the challenge; is the primary idea that draws everyone to the book. But once people realize the cost involved: reading, assessing their relationship, communicating every day for 30 days and yes ultimately understanding that "oneness" comes from Christ, we realize that we will lose those not committed to the entirety of what we believe is a Biblical journey to intimacy.

Yet, for those who do not believe, we hope that you will still read this book and proceed with the **30daysexchallenge.** Give it your best effort for the full 30 days; then, judge for yourselves if your relationship has improved. We would love to hear from you either way.

INTRODUCTION

This is Day 10 into the **30daysexchallenge**, and I am mentally, emotionally, and physically exhausted! Not from the challenge mind you but from the rigors of writing this book! Every time I lay down to rest, thoughts start racing through my head, and I cry out to God that I just can't get up and go back to my little lap-top! If you could only see it placed carefully on our bar in the kitchen with the cord draped ever so lightly around and across the screen. It somewhat inhibits my view, but this thing is hanging on by a small wire that could snap at any juncture. I have to jiggle it once in a while just to keep it from shutting down completely! Still, I am compelled to get up and continue writing. As I wrestle against the idea, I hear Him whisper in a loving, gentle voice: "I went through so much more than exhaustion, and I know you can make it."

I am not claiming this work to be "inspirational" or "God-breathed," but I do know that God will not let me rest until its completion. For whatever plan and purpose He deems, I continue to write. So, I do emphatically say this story is highly motivated by God and not Paul or I, although we are the main characters. And what "characters" we are.

Another motivation to write our story is the high divorce rate. We believe God is for marriage. We recognize that most divorces end due to what society has labeled as "irreconcilable differences". One or the other partner has decided that they "are not sorry" or "they can't forgive," or possibly both. We are writing to those who are married.

God's heart from the beginning of time is and always will be: first, a reconciliation to Himself, through the forgiveness of our sins by the work that Jesus did when He went to the cross; secondly, a reconciliation of our marriages through the acknowledgement of our sin and being sorry one to the other and then the conscious act of forgiving one another. This is our message of God's plan for the individual and His plan for our marriages.

Since we recognize the fact that many will not read an entire book written about marriage, we have a short acrostic to help those who may be apprehensive of the endeavor. Sex is the acrostic, appropriately. I know "e" is not "x", but we'll make it work for our purposes.

S –   Spiritual oneness
E –   Education and Effort
X –   Execute the plan for a better marriage and
        ultimately a better sex life!

The pathway to a greater sex life with your partner begins with our spiritual man first. We must be spiritually right with one another in order to fully please each other. If there is anything that is "between" a couple, such as unforgiveness, resentment, bitterness, hurt, unresolved issues, then spiritual oneness cannot be achieved. The old verse in the Bible teaches us, *"don't let the sun go down while you are still angry." Ephesians 4:26(NLT)* This Biblical principle means to make sure that there is nothing hindering your spiritual oneness.

Secondly, educate yourselves about marriage. We have created a system that defines marital behavior that we call "Scripts"; however, there are many other options available. (Some suggested reading is available on our website, www.**30daysexchallenge**.com.) Marriage takes work, so educate yourself and put forth the effort to make your marriage relationship the best that it can be.

Finally, execute your plan. Without a plan, our best intentions will fail.

Habits can be formed in less than 30 days. So, what would happen if couples practiced pleasing each other and rediscovering what makes each other happy for 30 days straight? This kind of commitment to your marriage can develop behavioral habits that can lead to a deepened relationship. Couples can find themselves spiritually one, effortlessly pleasing each other because their love has increased, and experiencing a healthier and more pleasurable sexual relationship. Obviously, this is the goal for the **30daysexchallenge**.

Paul and I have jointly written our story and, since we are fully one, believe that God will use all of the compilation of our thoughts and beliefs to help you. The following is a portion of the first message given by Paul at Relevant (our church in Tampa, Florida) in our **30daysexchallenge** series.

30daysexchallenge Message Series
Excerpts from "Business Time"
Pastor Paul Wirth

I know what some of you are thinking. Sex for 30 days? Are you kidding me?

I trust that you will stick with us, because I think that over the next 30 days many, if not all, of our relationships are going to be revolutionized. I want to guide you through what this whole thing looks like from a married couple's perspective and from the Bible.

I think it is ironic that the buzz going around Relevant, and the nation, is that all of the married couples are saying they don't think they can have sex for thirty days, and many of the singles are saying they cannot stop having sex for thirty days!

This is one of the many reasons why I believe Americans' sex lives are broken and shattered. We are like an old nursery rhyme. "Humpty Dumpty sat on a wall. Humpty Dumpty had a great fall. All the King's horses and all the King's men couldn't put Humpty together again.[1]"Our relationships are broken, and we cannot seem to make them whole again. Our Humpty Dumpty sex lives have left us fragile and fearful. We have lost too many pieces along the way to gather ourselves up, because deep down we believe that we are doomed to stumble all over again. Although our cultural exposure to sex has heightened over the past 10 years, it seems our level of personal satisfaction has plummeted, thus we play the old Rolling Stones song in our head: "I Can't Get No Satisfaction."

I know that there are some who do not think that the church should talk about sex because it is so personal and it is too risky. But, unfulfilling sex is one of the leading causes cited in divorce cases today, and going to church does not exempt you from the current statistics that estimate over 50% of all marriages end in divorce. If so many of us are living these unsatisfied lives, maybe we should take some time to find out why.

Another reason people don't think the church should talk about sex is because of the way the church has spoken about it in the past.

If we are listening to the early theologians of the church, then no wonder we are a bit confused. You see here is what the religious fathers said about sex. Much of what is taught in the church is based on those early Christian beliefs. I have paraphrased a few quotes from early religious leaders:

Augustine said: sex is ok, but passion and desire were sins.[2]

Thomas Aquinas said: as long as sex was not enjoyed, then marriage was ok.[3]

Martin Luther said: intercourse is never without sin, but God excuses it by His grace because the estate of marriage is His work.[4]

I believe another reason we need to tackle this subject is that, along with living in a post-modern society, we are also living in a post-marriage society. Marriage is looked upon as the problem, not the solution, to our relationships.

Because of the risqué nature of the topic, I have received many e-mails condemning this series. Some people have expressed to me that they believe God doesn't care about our sex lives. I think most people in the church have forgotten that God is the one who created us and that means that He created our sex organs. He then told Adam and Eve to use them.

If the Bible talks about sex, and it does, then we are going to talk about it. In fact, The Song of Songs is an entire book of the Bible that talks about sex and romance. God brought this whole idea of sex up just 28 verses into the Bible. Take a look at this verse with me:

Gen 1:28 (NLT)
[28]God blessed them and told them, "Multiply and fill the earth and subdue it. Be masters over the fish and birds and all the animals."

I don't think Adam and Eve came out of the bushes and said "God, guess what we can do?" Sex was His idea, and I believe that it is time to turn off the noise and tune in to a new channel that may just help us rediscover the passion and joy we once shared with our spouse. I know some of you may be saying, "But, Paul, sex for 30 days! Isn't that extreme?"

Some others of you may be saying, "I cannot do that, so forget the whole thing." If you don't even try, you will totally miss the point of this challenge by stopping before you start. Please know that this series is far more about healthy relationships than it is about sex. We really want people to understand each other at their deepest level. The problem is that most couples have stopped connecting on the sexual level, which is the most intimate way God has provided for us to connect.

I do believe that sex is reserved for the marriage bed, because this is where God has established a covenant. Not a contract or a commitment, but a covenant. And, there is a big difference between a covenant and a commitment.

I Corinthians 7:1-5a (NLT)

¹Now about the questions you asked in your letter. Yes, it is good to live a celibate life. ²But because there is so much sexual immorality, each man should have his own wife, and each woman should have her own husband. ³The husband should not deprive his wife of sexual intimacy, which is her right as a married woman, nor should the wife deprive her husband. ⁴The wife gives authority over her body to her husband and the husband also gives authority over his body to his wife. ⁵So do not deprive each other of sexual relations. The only exception to this rule would be the agreement of both husband and wife to refrain from sexual intimacy for a limited time, so they can give themselves more completely to prayer.

Now let's not change the headache excuse for the next 30 days to the prayer excuse.

Let me give you a little background on the idea of Biblical Covenants.

Covenants are forever.

Covenants were created by God.

Here is a list of what happened before a covenant took place:

- Family issues were addressed
- What was expected to be gotten out of the relationship from each side was discussed
- Who was going to be responsible for what was determined
- And who was responsible for the financial needs was also discussed and determined

These issues were discussed before the covenant was established by the families because of the problems that could have arisen in their culture.

Covenant relationships were based on the Hebrew word "dsx", which is translated "checed." (Pronounced: kheh'-sed) Checed described God's love towards humanity in the Old Testament. The definition of checed is goodness, kindness, and faithfulness.[5]

Yet this type of love is not the familiar love that we know. Checed cannot actually be translated verbatim into the English language; however, the word has been interpreted as "deeds of devotion", "loving kindnesses", "loyal deeds", and "unchanging love."[6]

You can see by the definition and by its interpretation why the word was used for God's love for His people. Checed love is the kind of love that most people expect to find in a marital relationship. Who doesn't want to receive "deeds of devotion", "loving kindness", "loyal deeds" and "unchanging love" from a spouse?

Hopefully, over the next 30 days, with God's help, we are going to change our relationships to the Checed version of love. We should not settle for the committed version of love that is so prevalent in our society today.

Through this series, we are going to track through a book of the Bible that may have been considered erotica back in its day. It is the book of Song of Songs. Here is how the book starts out:

Song of Songs 1:2-4 (MSG)
[2]Kiss me—full on the mouth! Yes! For your love is better than

wine, [3]*headier than your aromatic oils. The syllables of your name murmur like a meadow brook. No wonder everyone loves to say your name!* [4]*Take me away with you! Let's run off together! An elopement with my King-Lover! We'll celebrate, we'll sing, we'll make great music. Yes! For your love is better than vintage wine. Everyone loves you—of course! And why not?*

So, a couple of days ago, knowing that we were heading into this **30daysexchallenge**, I thought I would begin trying this whole idea of checed love.

I got up early with the kids and got them off to school while Susie was still sleeping. I know what you are saying, "that isn't that much." But, wait, there is more.

I noticed that the house was a bit untidy (Okay, it was a wreck!), so I decided to clean the house - the whole house: floors, bathrooms, kitchen, plus a whole lot more.

Well, when I got home, Susie kissed me "full on the mouth". I had no idea that cleaning the house was going to excite her so much. I find myself strangely drawn to housework these days.

How many of you men have had your wife kiss you full on the mouth lately? Wouldn't that be great if they would? Why do our sex lives as married couples seem to be struggling? I believe that it has more to do with our lack of understanding each other than it has to do with a lack of libido. There are some key principles that I think we men are going to have to understand if we are going to have our wives excited about this **30daysexchallenge**.

First, sex is more than just intercourse. My number one question to you is, "Have you created an environment of love, care, and security for your wife?"

Secondly, do you understand the Biblical view of the sexual union?

The New Testament teaches us that our sexual union is a picture of our oneness with Christ.

Ephesians 5:31-33 (NLT)
[31]*As the Scriptures say, "A man leaves his father and mother and is joined to his wife, and the two are united into one."* [32]*This is a great mystery, but it is an illustration of the way Christ and the church are one.* [33]*So again I say, each man must love his wife as he loves himself, and the wife must respect her husband.*

Over the next 30 days we are encouraging each of you, both male and female, to discover what it is that makes your spouse tick, so to speak. We want to build an environment of authentic "Checed" within our marriages - a loving caring, and secure environment in which to please each other. We will give each of you practical, everyday exercises that will help you as a couple to achieve this goal. (See Appendix A)

Most of us take our love for granted. We live busy lives. The jobs, kids, and busyness of our lives just get in the way.

This next passage explains how we take our love for granted:

Proverbs 5:15-19a (MSG)
[15]*Do you know the saying, "Drink from your own rain barrel, draw water from your own spring-fed well"?* [16]*It's true. Otherwise, you may one day come home and find your barrel empty and your well polluted.* [17]*Your spring water is for you and you only, not to be passed around among strangers.* [18]*Bless your fresh-flowing fountain! Enjoy the wife you married as a young man!* [19]*Lovely as an angel, beautiful as a rose-don't ever quit taking delight in her body. Never take her love for granted!*

Men: Over the next 30 days I want you to pretend like you are back in school trying to make the principal's honor roll and study your wife like never before.

Women: I want you to do the same with your husbands.

As you both connect with each other intimately, we want to make sure you are truly doing those things that please each other. Our goal is to help you discover how you are wired and, in doing so, why you act and react the way that you do to each other. We pray that this challenge will change the atmosphere of your relationship. We believe it is vitally important to understand each other. To that end, there are questions and personal assessments for each person to take at the end of the study to help you reach these goals.

With that said, let's begin the journey to an incredible 30 days of intimacy. We'll start with our own story and how the **30daysexchallenge** revitalized our marriage.

PART ONE:
"OUR STORY...FULLY EXPOSED"

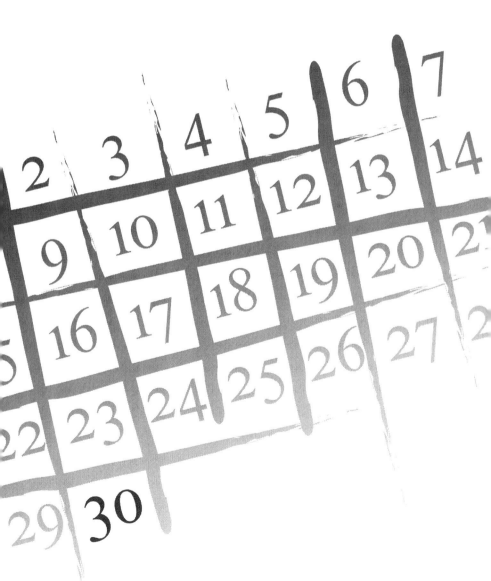

As I contemplate exposing our dirty laundry, two important factors compel me to write: God saved our marriage. And, there is so much more to say about the **30daysexchallenge** than just the mechanics of how to accomplish it.

Paul was born and raised in Tampa, grew up with wonderful loving parents that raised him to be a Christian from a small child. I, much like Paul, was raised in a very conservative Christian home, the daughter of a Baptist preacher. We both met at a very conservative Christian college, fell in love and ….

How we got from that point in our lives to the **30daysexchallenge** and world-wide attention is only well... A God thing!

I've known for a long time that God would have me write our love story, but I haven't felt motivated to actually do it for many reasons.

I guess the two primary reasons are our two beautiful children. I would never want to expose the greatest gifts that God has given us to any uncertain pain or distress.

Secondly, the last thing on earth that I want to do is hurt my husband in any way or fashion. He, too, is wonderful and loves me with a love that continues to grow and astound me.

So why now, one may ask?

Why not? We have the media's attention, so why not publish a book? I, too, wrestled with our reasons for publishing now, but I have come to a point in my life that I know people will make accusations and judge regardless of whether or not they have all of the facts. The blog world is proof of that.

Paul and I are so committed to this thing called marriage and its success that I just have to tell our story. Our prayer and hope is that our story and what we have learned from our mistakes will help marriages. This challenge is not just for couples who are struggling. Healthy marriages will benefit from the prioritization of intimacy that comes with committing to the challenge. The significance of our story lies directly in the challenge. It is the foundation and cornerstone of what we have to offer you as a couple.

With that said, we are fully exposed.

THE DRIFT:

In the beginning of our relationship, we had that kind of "goofy grin" that some call the "look of love." We all try to play it off like we don't act or look that way; but, when it comes right down to it, true love does start out with that romantic gaga acting stage. In fact, my family caught me on video with the gaga stage. It was back in the early 90's when the handheld video camera was selling like hot cakes. I remember I was in our upstairs bathroom brushing my teeth and awaiting the arrival of Paul, who I had not seen for a whopping whole week! He was driving all the way from Tampa to Indiana (an 18-hour drive) just to be with me over the holidays and to ask my father for my hand in marriage. My brother-in-law had gotten the camera as a present from his parents for Christmas, and he was filming almost everything!

As I was brushing my teeth, he came around the corner and asked if I was excited to see Paul. I replied, in a goofy voice, "He's the most wonderful man in the world!" We had been great friends the previous semester and had taken a few drama classes together. He would flirt with me during class and then take his umbrella to pick up his girlfriend. I was pretty much over the initial attention that he had given me by that summer, but I wrote him a friendly letter just to see how he was doing. He later told me that he received a letter the same day from his girlfriend, but he found himself opening my letter first. Paul and I had a great friendship, and it continued when we went back to school in the fall. In the first few days of being back at college, his girlfriend told him that she had to leave for the semester to help at home with some familial problems. He told me it was over between them, and I guess there wasn't much substance to their relationship anyway. We really didn't start dating right away. In fact, most of my friends thought that he was interested in my baby sister who had just started college as a freshman.

It was my senior year, and I had always been serious about not dating unless I thought they could possibly be "potential mate" material. I really didn't date much at all in college. Now Paul, on the other hand, was what we term today as a "playa". Well, not really, but as much as one could be a "playa" in a little conservative Christian college. One night it was storming, as it does frequently in Chattanooga, and I didn't have an umbrella to walk to the dining hall. I called Paul up and asked him to come and walk me to dinner with his umbrella. This is when he swears that I was interested in him as more than just a good friend, but, since I am writing the story, I am sticking to my rendition, and I really just didn't want to get wet!

A few days later it seemed as if we were spending much of our free time together, and he finally asked me to go on an official date! At first it was great. We were such great friends that it just seemed natural. I remember he took me to one of the many Civil War parks in the area. As we were hiking, he took my hand. Now, that was where the oddness struck. I was taken back a bit but knew that our friendship was strong. I guess we started a physical attraction for each other that has never been extinguished. We got engaged that January and spent the next college semester apart. He moved home to save up some money, and I completed my four-year degree. We were married on May 19, 1990.

So, just how does all of this lead to the **30daysexchallenge?**

About 8 years into our marriage, Paul and I got caught by the "drift". I call it the drift because it is like a wave gently pulling a raft rider out – first, he goes 3 feet, then 5. Then, when he's about 30 feet down the shore, he looks up from his relaxing moment to discover: "I'm not where I once was…"

I believe the drift is one identifiable cause of our "terrible" marriage. Recognize it and your smart in your relationship. But, for most of us, it is called the drift because we don't recognize it until the damage is done. You, too, look up in a moment of despair to discover that, "We're not where we once were….and how did we get down here?"

I believe that any relationship left to itself will experience a drift. Knowing what I know now, Paul and I were not smart about our relationship. We simply felt so secure in our "bond of Christian marriage," that we failed to recognize the change that was happening. Life happens and, as our story goes, we were quite successful in our careers. On the outside things "appeared" grand.

During this time, we fought a lot behind closed doors so that we could keep up the appearances that we felt were expected of a youth pastor. We just thought that "things are as good as they get!" After all, no one is perfect right?

Sadly, even those closest to us didn't talk about relationships too much. I remember at our previous church there was a young couples' marriage study that all of our youth workers attended. I wondered why we were never invited to join in, but I assume now that the leaders must have thought we had a great marriage because we were in pastoral leadership. Whatever their reasoning, and our reasoning for not pursuing a stronger marital relationship, we were totally filled with the busyness of our lives.

Five years into our marriage, we decided we were ready to start our family. We had a difficult time conceiving. Having a baby was not as easy as it seemed. All of the other couples we knew wanted a baby and within a few months easily conceived a child.

After a year of the roller-coaster of trying every month to conceive, we finally got pregnant. Sadly, it was a tubal pregnancy that ended in a miscarriage.

Wow, that was our first significant "hurt" in our married lives. Oh, by the way, we married at the ripe old age of 22! Moving on…

Me, being the impatient one….well, hummm, both of us being impatient, we immediately tried for another baby. After all, our never-wavering, strong faith in God got us through the loss of our first baby. One month later, the fertility stick showed double lines! We were very excited, but cautious.

Finally, on March 3, 1996, our beautiful red-headed porcelain doll was born. Even though she was considered a borderline preemie, the doctors did not appear alarmed. We felt enormously blessed just to have our precious baby in our arms.

In the midst of the happiest days of our personal lives things started strangely unraveling at our church. Paul's God-given ability to lead and determination were very evident even as a young youth pastor. Yet, just as the youth group seemed about to explode with growth, some of our church leadership began questioning the integrity of our lead pastor. Several months of "he said, she said" and late night business meetings all came to a head one Sunday when our lead pastor and his wife stood in front of our church and resigned.

It was a very ugly experience, an experience that crept back into our thoughts and lives over the next couple of years.

Another hurt. This one led to a move: a new city, a new church, and new challenges for our relationship.

About a year into our move, we came to the realization that our daughter just wasn't meeting the expected growth benchmarks. You know the ones laid out in "What to Expect When You're Expecting"; followed by the thorough: "What to Expect the First Year". I always found it humorous that they just quit after the toddler/pre-school year. Did they just give up on parents? Did they decide, if they ain't got it by now, they are NEVER gonna get it?

Our little "Fee Fee", as Papa (Paul's father) proudly endears her, just wasn't measuring up. Despite all of the affirmations from experienced parents all around us who said, "She is just a late bloomer" and "She is going to be just fine", we finally took her to the neurologist. We were not shocked when the doctor let us know that she was "developmentally delayed." Paul says that the doctor told us that day that she was mildly mentally retarded, but I don't remember him saying that.

While this would turn out to be a huge hurt in our lives initially, in our ignorance, we wondered why we spent the money to hear the doctor say what we already knew. Anyone who spent time with her knew that she was "developmentally delayed!"

God was so gracious in our lives during this time. He eased us into the realization that Ashlyn is mentally handicapped. Well, I say ease now. There was one exceptionally hard encounter. One person emphatically pronounced to me: "You do KNOW that Ashlyn is mentally retarded!!!" I know she was only trying to awaken us out of our denial, but really, a little compassion would have been nice.

I so hate that word "retarded". For some reason it is coming back into our coarse jesting and meaningless chatter. I was teaching music at a local school recently and, in back-to-back classes, two different kids used the word derogatorily. People have no idea what they are saying when they blurt out that someone is "retarded!" Most of the time when friends use the term and catch themselves, they immediately apologize. We usually are not bothered by the use of the word, but sometimes, if you catch us on the wrong day, it is difficult to overlook.

This hurt, obviously, is one that is ever present in our lives and relationship. We know that if we did not have God in our lives we could not bear the heaviness of caring and raising this golden little princess.

People often ask just what Ashlyn's diagnosis is because her outward appearance does not suggest that anything is wrong.

Yes, but herein lies the rub....because she really does not appear to be handicapped, she just looks like an unruly child! Live with that one and let that fact settle in a bit.

I guess as an external emotional protection mechanism, we have mastered how to operate in public. I call it being blessed with "non-observance." When in Target, I don't give or receive eye contact. It helps tremendously, except for those rare occasions when confronted head on with it. I remember an instance a couple of years ago. It was a Saturday morning, and we were rushing to get to one of the biggest church events that we do each year.

We absolutely had to be on time for the morning family event because, after a certain hour, we had to pay admission to enter. I was hurrying to Wal-Mart so we could have an additional game for the kids. I wanted to buy some bamboo poles and some fishing string. Anyone that has been to a kids festival knows that the fishing game is a must have. As I was driving, Ashlyn muttered something about her puzzle and the pool. After deciphering just what she was trying to tell me, I realized that she had thrown her jig-saw puzzle into our swimming pool. That didn't go over too well as anyone would imagine. Filters are built for small dirt particles, not 500 piece jig-saw puzzles!

I turned the van around and headed back to the house, swept out the puzzle mess, jumped back into the van, and made my way to Wal-Mart. Ashlyn was around 10 years old and very big for her age, but she was out of sorts and I was out of time. I threw her into a cart and darted down the aisles to find my bamboo poles.

Not five minutes later, poles and fishing line in hand, I made my way to the front of the store. That's when a young manager stopped me and told me that I had to remove Ashlyn from the cart because she was too big to ride in the back. Of course, I just smiled and raced to the check out saying, "I'm finished now". I didn't have time to stop and explain our issues to this kid manager. But he proceeded to chase me down and demanded, "I mean now, ma'am!" I just turned around and yelled, "She is special needs" and kept on rollin'!

Of course, I lost it all and the tears began to fall right in front of the cashier, who sympathetically asked, "Are you ok?" I explained the entire incident, and she assured me that he had no business telling me what to do. Her kindness made me feel a little better. This is just one instance that I can only now look back on, and I just shake my head.

But, I did make it to our Family Event on time!

Still, for the most part, I just tell people that raising Ashlyn is much like living with Rainman, Radio, and I am Sam - all wrapped up into one beautiful curly haired redhead.

So, back to those early years, our relationship was, at best, held together by companionship and only sealed by our faith. Once a little "special needs" child was added to the mix, voilà! Can you say "train wreck?" Our relationship spiraled down quickly during this time in our lives. I was at home consumed with Fee Fee, and Paul was working hard to grow another youth ministry. We both were going our separate ways, just doing our own thing. I can see now that there was definitely a lack of intimacy between us, but strangely enough, not a lack of sex. During this time we had gotten pregnant not once, but twice! Sadly, both ended in miscarriages... back-to-back miscarriages.

I know I am starting to sound like Job! Seriously it does get better, but, unfortunately, not before it gets worse!

The hurts just kept piling up. I know my pain in losing those babies was bearable because I firmly believe that God is in control, and those babies are in Heaven.

Still, dealing with the challenges of a mentally handicapped child became overwhelming! She didn't speak. Instead, she screamed and cried to get her needs met. We suffered with sleep deprivation because she woke up every night and would not go back to sleep. Life was exhausting, and we had little support at that time in our lives.

In addition to all that, we carried hurts from our last church ministry that had never really healed.

Paul was especially affected; he really missed a couple of close friends and his hometown. With all of these components in our lives running rampant, we both "escaped" from our struggles, each in our own way. God seemed distant at that time. We kept saying and teaching what we knew to be the truth about God and relationships but not living what we believed. Our marriage degenerated dramatically.

At first, the distance became sort of familiar to me. But as time passed, my woman's intuition sensed a change that indicated we were doing more than just growing apart.

REPENTANCE:

God never lets His children continue in sin without making a great effort to bring them back to Himself.

In our case, God used a fellow youth worker. When I told her about Paul's strange behaviors, she and her husband confronted Paul that afternoon with their concerns.

As I remember it (It has been over 10 years now), only a few hours later, Paul and I were driving home. I began asking some prob-ing questions. It was then that he began to reveal to me the truth about his distance.

He was very broken about it and, what we call in church world, "repentant."

In the hours that followed his confession, Paul refused to leave me alone. Even when I would go into another room, he would come in and wipe away my tears. He gently pleaded, with tears in his eyes, "I'm sorry. I never wanted to hurt you. Please forgive me." I know that it was God's plan for him to experience all of the pain and tears that his unfaithfulness had caused me. I forgave him for his unfaithfulness, and he would comfort me over and over and continue to tell me how sorry he was that he had hurt me.

Paul is a very tender-hearted man, and I am so thankful to God for that. I am certain that his tenderness was, in part, from his love for his Lord and for what Paul had done through this sin against Him as well. By the next weekend, we had gone to our lead pastor and confessed everything. We resigned from the church.

Our church gave us the opportunity to say we were sorry before the congregation that following Sunday night. Yes, "we" apologized. As a couple, I knew in my heart that I, too, had contributed to this immoral relationship. I knew my part in my head, but later we learned the right terminology. One author calls it "meeting your spouse's emotional needs". The Bible calls it "pleasing" each other. Neither of us were doing either well.

I remember in the spring of that year, Paul had tried to communicate to me that he needed more sexual fulfillment. I remember telling him that "I guess this is as good as it gets." Interestingly, as we later felt the need to unpack the entire thing, his affair was never about love. It was entirely about unmet sexual fulfillment.

It is interesting how our minds remember significant experiences in our lives as if they happened yesterday. I remember feeling a sense of relief along with joy. Which at first sounds a bit strange, but God had placed in my heart the story about the Father and the Prodigal Son. The son had squandered all of this inheritance and had stooped to the lowest of lows as a human being; still, when the son came walking up the path to his home, the hopeful father was waiting at the top of the hill.

He had stood at that same place, day after day, just waiting for his son to return home to him. When the father recognized his wayward son, he ran to meet him, grabbed him into his arms and loved him back into the family. (Luke 15:11-31)

While those in the church were experiencing feelings of anger, disappointment, and sadness, I was really feeling joy that night. My husband, my lover, and my friend – my Prodigal - had come home! His heart had been turned far away from us for a season, but now he was home. In spite of the hurt, I was so happy that his heart was home.

I remember that last church service so vividly. I recall standing next to Paul at the pulpit as he remorsefully let the church know he was wrong and how sorry he was for his actions. I remember the looks on those teenagers' faces, sitting just off of the center front of the church. It was very disappointing for everyone. The one thing that I said emphatically was, "many couples would split-up over such an affair, but I choose love." And, by God's grace, we did choose love. Against all odds, God's love was enough to help us make it.

After the service, many people greeted us warmly and told us that they would be praying for us. One member even told Paul that God would use him again in the ministry. I know that little church in Virginia did pray for us, as did many other people in our family.

When we walked out to the parking lot to get into our car, I remember looking at Paul and asking him how he felt. His words are still etched in my heart today. He stopped and said, "I feel a heavy weight has been lifted off of my shoulders. I think this was good closure for us." It was good for all of us.

We have since visited that church a few times over the years and still talk to dear friends we met during our time there. We have even been contacted over the years by some of the youth. So many times ministers just disappear and nothing is stated publicly, so the congregants are left to wonder and speculate. I have talked to many adults who said that in their teenage years they had a youth pastor do the same thing, but the church swept it under the carpet and they never had a chance to say good-bye. I am so thankful for the wisdom of the elders of that church.

When we returned to Tampa, Paul and I met with a few counselors. Each encouraged us to continue loving and forgiving each other. They also encouraged us to try and identify the root of the problem – why this all happened.

We discussed it a lot. As we talked, Paul explained to me that the enemy would play the movie just so far in his head… but the ending with all of the ugly consequences would never be revealed. As a result, he would just see the great parts, the fun, but never the tragedy, pain, and loss. We also discovered that we had so much hurt in our lives that our "drift" had left empty spaces. Those spaces left open doors, allowing us to be filled by others and by things, instead of by each other.

RECONCILIATION:

God always knows what we need before we need it. As a result, we already had planned to take a week's vacation at home in Tampa. The morning after that evening church service, we started home. On the long drive home, I ended up driving into the late hours of the night. Ashlyn was sleeping (the car was always a good place for her to sleep), and Paul was resting as well. I remember so clearly how, in that drive home, God spoke to my heart. It was almost an audible voice. It was so clear that I remember it verbatim to this day. He spoke gently and softly and posed this question: "Susie, if I can forgive him, then how can you do less?"

I know I already said that I had forgiven him, but, as humans, something happens when we are hurt so deeply that we are cut to the core of our very being. We have a very difficult time "forgetting". So, in those hours and days after the confession, I would think of questions and wanted to know when, where - all the details. Week after week, I would awake in the middle of the night thinking about them together and every kind of imagination that goes along with it all. I even had dreams that Paul left us, and I would wake up in a cold sweat - distraught and emotional. Again, Paul would comfort me and ask for forgiveness.

But, in that drive home, I knew that if Jesus could forgive him- forgive his hands, his feet, and every part of his being. Then, how could I do less? You see, from a young child I had been taught the Biblical principle that instructs us to forgive even as we have been forgiven.

"You must make allowance for each other's faults and forgive the person who offends you. Remember, the Lord forgave you, so you must forgive others." Col. 3:13a (NLT)

I knew Christ had forgiven me of much in my life. Who's to say that it could have been Paul as the victim and me as the un-faithful spouse?

We all have it in us. We are all very capable in ourselves, and we are all just a step away from it. But, by God's grace, it wasn't me.

Still, I had to learn how to forgive - not just once, but often. As I did, God healed my broken heart. As thoughts would race into my mind, I would quickly diffuse them and whisper: "No, I have already forgiven that". I would then quote the Scripture again, "I forgive even as I have been forgiven." I learned to walk in that verse.

It was hourly at first, then often during the course of a day. Finally, there was a day that I didn't even think about it at all! God is so good. I had always heard the phrase, "time heals all hurts." I emphatically believe now that, "God heals all hurts."

When we arrived in Tampa that next day, we sat Paul's parents down and told them. They immediately sent us to the beach for a week alone. They kept "Fee Fee" with them. This was totally a "God thing".

On our way to the beach, we stopped at the local Christian bookstore desperately looking for SOMETHING to help us get through this. I remember looking through the marriage section when a title just popped out at me. The book was entitled, "Surviving an Affair" by Dr. Willard Harley, Jr. He is also the author of "His Needs, Her Needs."

I called Paul over and we both emphatically said, "This is it, let's get this." This is where the next, and best, chapter of our story begins.

We took the next couple of days and read through the pages. It was incredible the accuracy of how we studied Dr. Harley's view that all affairs are basically the same. The difference is that some are "emotional" and others are "sexual." He explained his plan and, amazingly, he states that the most successful couples that recover from affairs are those that are able to get away and begin healing and intimacy for.....you guessed it! 30 days![7]

Now don't jump to conclusions and close the book just yet. Life gets better...oh sooo much better!

One key note, Paul and the pastoral team at Relevant did not consider Dr. Harley's 30-day plan when they came up with the

30daysexchallenge. In fact, it wasn't until a radio interview that the light turned on for Paul. The radio personality asked the question, "Where did the **30daysexchallenge** all start?"

After Paul mentioned it started initially from our broken marriage over 10 years ago, the interviewer asked Paul, "So did you have 30 days of sex then?" Paul replied, "As a matter of fact, I hadn't really thought about it before, but yes." While we had forgotten about the 30 days of intimacy (a period which, we believe, God divinely orchestrated in order for our relationship to heal), God had not!

The intimacy of being alone together for 30 days was one of the key factors in re-building our broken marriage at that time." Now that could only be a "God thing!"

Just to clarify one point. No, we didn't stay at the beach for 30 days. We actually went back to Virginia, packed up our belongings for three weeks, and put a for-sale sign in the yard.

We headed back to Tampa with no job or income - only hope and a prayer…a prayer that God would be faithful to us even when we were not faithful to Him. We moved in with Paul's parents. They owned a little two bedroom one bath home with less than 1100 sq ft of living area. This was the second time in our married life that we lived with them! But, now there were three of us moving in with the two of them. It was interesting to say the least. His parents bought a futon with an upgraded mattress, and we stayed in what Floridians call the "Florida Room," usually an addition off the back of the house. They wanted me to be comfortable, since the five would soon be six! Yes, during all this, I had gotten pregnant (Ok, not during the 30 days!)

Amazingly, I had conceived sometime in the middle of all the mess. By the end of the year, God had sold our house, by owner. We didn't even lose any money. In fact, we made money on it. The lawyer kept telling us how fortunate we were, and we knew it was only a "God thing." During this time, we experienced one of the greatest moments in our lives: we found out that we were having a boy!

I wasn't looking at the ultra-sound. I had my eyes fixed upon Paul. The expression on his face when the nurse announced, "looks like it's going to be a boy", was unforgettable. God blessed us with a new home, and we moved just two weeks before Anthony was born. The year and a half in that little house was such an oasis. I called it my "haven." God got Paul an incredible job where he only worked between 2-3 days a week and was home the rest of the time. It was just the recipe that we needed to keep our relationship growing in the right direction. In the greatness of these months, we were so happy. Still, there was something missing.

Paul had loved being a pastor of teenagers, and I loved being in ministry along with him. We were just not sure if God was ever going to allow us the opportunity to minister vocationally again. We started a small Bible study for young married couples in our neighborhood. God was using us and had given us this time to completely restore our relationship and heal our marriage. Soon after we started our home study, Paul felt peace about starting to look for a position in a church again.

RESTORATION:

We didn't even know if a church would take a chance on hiring us ever again after our past failures. In fact, our experience had been that, once you blow it, you are done with vocational ministry. We even had spiritual advisors, whom we loved and trusted, tell us, "Paul, now don't even think about ever getting back into ministry. And Susie, you are probably going to have to work now to help make ends meet!"

On more than one occasion, we walked away from our friends feeling beat down and under condemnation. I just wasn't going to believe that my loving God was into that. However, I am not ignorant of the Scriptures. In Proverbs 6:32-33 (NLT) the Bible talks about the "shame" that follows anyone who is unfaithful and the far-reaching effects even to his family forever.

But, the Scripture also says, *"He made Him who knew no sin to be sin on our behalf, so that we might become the righteousness of God in Him" 2 Corinthians 5:21 (NASB),* which means that we no longer have to live under condemnation or wear a "scarlet letter," since Jesus makes us righteous with God.

When God forgives us, He removes our sins. *"He has removed our sins as far as the east is from the west." Psalm 103:12 (NLT)* When we are in Christ and forgiven by his blood, the blood that HE so willingly gave on the cross, He makes us righteous before God. Not anything we do, but what He did. I held close to my heart the Truths of those Scriptures. Paul had been broken and repentant. I knew in my heart that that counted significantly to God!

I am not making light of the severe consequences that go along with immorality and the lasting consequences that our sin had on the youth in Virginia. It hurts my heart to think about it all to this day. Still, God has been very gracious in allowing us to see His work in some of those young people in spite of our failures as role models to them. You see it never is about the man as much as it is about God. We fail, but God never fails! That is a huge lesson I have learned, and one we all should heed. We are human, and we fail. God is the only unfailing love.

33

Another lesson that God has taught us over and over again is that when God restores, He restores completely and that means positional restoration, too.

What some people fail to understand is that God doesn't take our gifts and calling away when we fail. He is in the business of complete restoration. For the next five plus years, we served at a great church in suburban Tampa, where God did some incredible things. God used our time at that ministry to launch us into the unknown of church planting! In the summer of 2004, Paul and I and two other couples met in our living room to pray about what God would have "Relevant Church" be. By the start of the **30daysexchallenge**, God had grown our six people into an average attendance of more than 350 on any given Sunday.

It is risky going big for God. Our lives have always been about risking it all for whatever He would have for us and our church. This full exposure of our past is another risk for God. Discretion and much prayer went into these risks. Still, the crux of our ministry has been based upon God's authentic work in our personal lives. You see, when you have a special needs child, you can't be anything other than just who you are. Our struggles are fully exposed where everyone can see...The good, the bad, and the ugly! Maybe that should have been the title of this piece.

I am not fearful or complaining about what God has called us to do, and I am ready for those who would trample down our love story, for I know there will be those that will.

Our prayer through all of this is that no one would miss the incredible picture that God has made of our lives. For us, it is a picture of "redemption" We are to be broken when we sin against God and our mates. God wants us to forgive each other in all things. He gently and softly reconciles us back to Himself and each other through this process of forgiveness; and, finally, He restores us to our calling.

Although redemption is a big Bible word, simply put, God the Father sent his son Jesus to rescue us from our sins so that we can be reconciled to God the Father through Jesus the Son. This is God's plan for us as individuals, and His plan for our families. He only asks of us to believe and receive Christ's forgiveness. *"If you confess with your mouth that Jesus is Lord and believe in your heart that God raised him from the dead, you will be saved."* Romans 10:9 (NLT)

Secondly, our love story is about saving marriages and families. We believe God has allowed us to go through so much and learn about how we forgive our spouses, and how we love our spouses through pleasing each other unconditionally and sacrificially as well, so that we can help those who are hurting. If we can make it, any marriage can make it!

Part two of our book, we pray, will help you understand how to forgive, love and learn more about yourself and your sexual relationship through four mini-challenges to 30 days of sex.

Our goal is that you will experience deeper and more meaningful intimacy as a result of the effort you make to complete the **30daysexchallenge**. We have also provided practical tools that we believe will guide you into a refreshing renewal of your marriage relationship. A brief preview of each of the mini-challenges to the **30daysexchallenge** is as follows:

Spiritual Challenge-

We believe that as we experience forgiveness by our God, then we are able to offer forgiveness to others by following Christ's example. We are also able to love unconditionally and sacrificially as we learn from Christ's example. Only then can spiritual healing take place in our relationship and "rightness" or spiritual oneness can occur.

Emotional Challenge-

In the emotional challenge the goal is to educate yourself. Your spouse is your textbook. This is done by identifying your "Script." A script is the couple's pattern of behavior toward each other. How they act and react, especially to conflicts but also to their general life together. In the emotional challenge, learning how to please each other in practical, everyday life is a Biblical command and skill that should cause feelings of love to rise between you and your spouse.

Sexual Challenge-

As we strive to love each other unconditionally and sacrificially by practically pleasing each other and putting each other first, our sexual relationship and the intimacy between us cannot help but be healthier. Prioritizing sexual intimacy for 30 days is the goal.

Physical Challenge-

As we work to keep our environment or "ethos" in harmony, our marriages and families can be healthier and happier. The physical steps produce the outward effects of our inward harmony, where the spiritual, emotional, and sexual are all operating right. Therefore, our environment or ethos is right. And all is right in the world. Well, at least in our intimate world.

PART TWO:
"THE CHALLENGE"

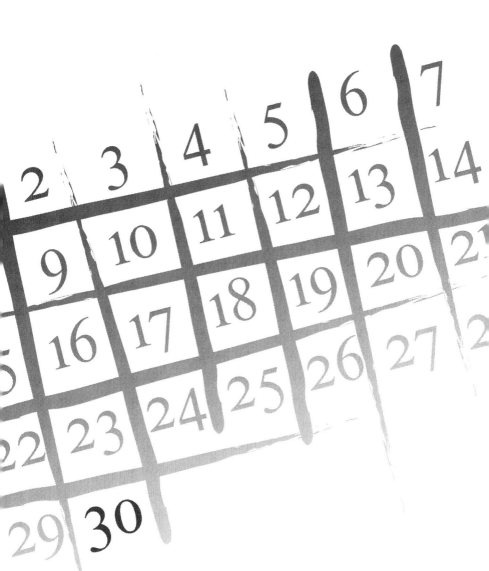

SPIRITUAL CHALLENGE

Our Scripts!

It is important that both people read this second half of the book together before starting their 30-day challenge. In Appendix A, there are 30 days of questions intended to start the 30 days of sexual intimacy and enhance the over-all process. We pray these questions will aid in making the challenge a success for you. After 18 plus years of marriage and all the trials that we have gone through, we have found that humor in our relationship is definitely medicine to our souls.

With that in mind, we compare our marriage relationship to the old movie "Ground Hog Day". You may remember the movie. Bill Murray awakens each morning only to realize that he is re-living the same day over and over again until, of course, he wins the girl. Because of our theatrical backgrounds, it seems like the most visual connection for us. We have noticed an uncanny sequence of the conflicts that naturally occur almost repeatedly throughout our marriage. It is like our life is our own version of Ground Hog Day. As we have talked with other couples and discussed this uncanny similarity, many have agreed that conflict in marriage, for the most part, revolves around the same issues. We are creatures of pattern. These issues may be silent for months; and, for whatever reason, they are set off again. Then, it's "Ground Hog Day!"

In order to help us easily identify our conflicts, we have labeled these recurring issues as our "Script". If you think about your own relationship and those things that cause the most disagreements, arguments, fights, then you will identify your "Script!" It is like you are participating in a live play and you both are the leading characters. The things you fight over are almost always the same things that just keep cycling back around in your lives. In our quest to learn more about each other and work on our marriage, we have learned that most of the time our Scripts are the result of our differences. What we argue and fight about, and how we fight or disagree, will often be the same. Think about your Script and focus on the cyclical issues in your relationship.

Write a few of the cyclical issues in your relationship in the following space:

_____

_____

_____

_____

_____

_____

_____

_____

_____

_____

_____

_____

_____

_____

_____

_____

_____

_____

_____

_____

_____

_____

_____

_____

Now that you have been introduced to your "Script", we want to offer you hope. Hope that you don't have to live Ground Hog Day over and over and over for the rest of your married lives. We know that hope for breaking the repetitive cycles of a relationship can only happen when two people are willing to work toward changing their Script. God has taught us that our differences, whatever they may be, often lead to conflict. Conflict which is not resolved leads to the tendency for your relationship to drift. Obviously, our relationship had drifted so far in the early years of our marriage that the decision to cross immoral boundaries was made. Since the drift zone is so dangerous, we want to make every effort to stay as close to one another as possible. In order to accomplish this, we try to practice the Biblical principle of going to bed with everything right between us. Even when our old Script creeps back into our lives, we immediately try to practice making up before we make love.

The first step in the **30daysexchallenge** begins with making up- forgiveness. It only makes sense that couples make up before making love. In our story (which I have now laid bare before the world), if Paul had not been sorry for his unfaithfulness to me, I honestly do not know where we would be right now. On the flip side, suppose he had been sorry yet I had chosen not to forgive him. However, because he was sorry and by God's grace I was able to forgive him, I believe God's healing happened for us.

The key point to understand is that it was a spiritual healing first and foremost. Paul and I have counseled many struggling couples. The success and failure of each relationship came down to both of the people being willing to ask forgiveness from their spouse and offer forgiveness to their spouse. If one spouse shuts down completely - emotionally and spiritually - to their spouse, the relationship almost always is irreconcilable. We have found that reconciliation takes two willing people who recognize their imperfections and failures as contributing factors as to where they have allowed their relationship to go. Both people must be willing to work at rekindling their love for one another.

Forgiveness is not easy. The only reason that I was able to completely forgive Paul and move to a point of reconciliation was because God directly pointed out to me that I had been forgiven when I didn't deserve forgiveness.

I am reminded of the story in the Bible when Jesus rushes to an adulterous woman's rescue. In Jewish culture a woman found guilty of adultery was often stoned to death for her transgression. In a quiet gentle manner, Jesus stooped down and drew a line in the sand. He submits to the accusers this poignant and powerful question: *"He who is without sin among you, let him be the first to throw a stone at her." I John 8:7b (NASB)*

This story points to a significant flaw in our human nature. We find it easy to judge others, even while we are ignoring much more significant faults in ourselves. As the Bible addresses in another passage, we have become experts at pointing out the speck in our neighbor's eye while we live with a log in our own. (Matthew 7:1-4)

As Christians, Paul and I believe that understanding and experiencing the forgiveness that Christ offers each person is the only way that we can learn to truly forgive.

It really is only through understanding the "Forgiver" that we are able to forgive completely even as Christ has forgiven us completely.

If you are searching for a change in your relationship, or maybe this is the first time that you fully comprehend the magnitude of what Christ did for you, would you consider accepting the forgiveness that God offers through His Son, Jesus?

The Bible states: *"God showed how much He loved us by sending His one and only Son into the world so that we might have eternal life through Him. This is real love-not that we loved God, but that He loved us and sent His Son as a sacrifice to take away our sins."* I John 4:9-10 (NLT)

We trust that you will begin this spiritual healing by experiencing God's forgiveness.

Secondly, and much harder, will be reconciliation with your spouse. In most relationships we fail each other frequently. You may have heard the old saying, "you always hurt the ones you love the most". Those failures have to be addressed or a relationship is not healthy. It is broken. In order to get back to loving each other rightly, forgiveness must take place.

Begin by asking if there is anything that needs to be forgiven. Yes, this may open "Pandora's Box," but this exercise is necessary, because we believe unforgiveness is the emotional equivalent to a physical infection. Anything that goes un-forgiven is like the oozing, pussing sore that does not heal until you've gotten the cell-killing agent out of the wound.

Some of our relationships are like infections, and they will get worse before they can get better. This first step is only for the brave but will prove to be the beginning of a rekindling that I pray will never be extinguished.

Some may need to have a mediator or counselor present to help uncover the infection. As with any wound, it will hurt. In fact, it may hurt a lot. But think of the alternative. Are you willing to allow the infection to continue and lead to the potential death of your relationship?

A great starting point is just saying: "I'm sorry and I was wrong for…"

Take the time to express your sorrow and failures to your partner in the spaces below.

_____

_____

_____

_____

_____

_____

_____

_____

_____

_____

_____

_____

_____

This should touch the heart of the one you love and get forgiveness rolling. However, if there are years of resentment and bitterness from unforgiveness (or worse), years of harbored ill feelings, it may take a while to prove that you truly are sorry. If this is the case for one or both of you, take time right now to express your extreme hurt and apprehension and express either verbally to your spouse or write how you are feeling in the following blanks. Be as specific as possible.

_____

_____

_____

_____

_____

_____

_____
_____
_____
_____
_____
_____
_____
_____
_____
_____
_____
_____
_____
_____

Another thought to consider: Ask yourself the question, "Am I truly sorry?" If you can't honestly see yourself as God sees you and agree with Him that you are full of yourself (sin) to your very core, then this challenge isn't for you.

We fear you will go to the same well where you have always gone. You will get the same thing from it that you have always gotten - a broken relationship.

If you can see your shortcomings and see yourself as God sees you, as a fallen person, then we believe your gut level honesty with God and your spouse will be the beginning point to reconciliation and ultimately rekindling the passion in your marriage. This is the same way that God saved our marriage over ten years ago.

For those of us that tend to be grudge holders, concentrate on the passage of Scripture that says,

"Make allowance for each other's faults, and forgive anyone who offends you. Remember, the Lord forgave you, so you must forgive others." Col. 3:13 (NLT)

Reciting this verse helps keep our minds and hearts focused on our own imperfections so that our expectations for others are not too high. It may be helpful to list a few of your own faults in the lines below and offer your forgiveness to your spouse as well:

_____

_____

_____

_____

_____

_____

_____

_____

_____

_____

_____

EMOTIONAL CHALLENGE

Your Way, Right Away

30daysexchallenge Message Series
Excerpts from "Your Way, Right Away"
Pastor Paul Wirth

Unfortunately, many of us treat our relationships like a fast food drive-thru window. We get up to the window and the female orders a romantic evening, flowers, and thought-provoking conversation. The men order up "Super-sized" sex! When we live out our lives wanting everything our way, right away, it can lead to some major problems, and most times it does.

I think we often believe that just because we love each other two individuals can come together in this thing called marriage and still expect to get what they want, when they want it.

When the honeymoon is over (and for some that is about 3 hours into the honeymoon), we discover that there is going to have to be some negotiations if we are going to make this thing called marriage work.

Our prayer is that all of us will gain a whole new perspective on how we place our drive-thru orders as it relates to our marriages.

However, just because you are armed with new knowledge does not necessarily mean that things are going to magically get better. One couple emailed us a few days into the challenge to let us know how things were going for them. They said that, as they were discussing the questions, his wife threw the book down in anger. She didn't like the response that he had given her. She said if they were going to fight and argue then she was not doing the challenge. The husband went on to say, "I guess we really do have some issues to resolve." He continued to thank us for listening to God and making the challenge available for everyone. As we read his signature, we realized the husband was the pastor of another church. No one is immune from marital conflict.

So, how do you deal with the conflict and continue to be intimate at the same time? We believe in order to end the mentality of "my way right away," two people need to order up some selflessness, and a big order of self-sacrifice!

I do not believe that any of us can give selflessly on a daily basis apart from the love of Christ. I say that because as human beings we may say we are going to put our spouse first until we feel like we are the only ones making the effort day after day. Then our humanity rises up and claims like Popeye…"I've taken all I can stanz and I can't stanz no more!" All of us have this natural tendency to put our own needs first. But, when we act as Christ acted toward us, we sacrifice even though we may not receive anything in return.

You see this whole challenge really boils down to learning some major skills that are necessary for renewing our relationships and building intimacy. Yet in order to learn any new skill, first we need to set an environment that is conducive to learning and favorable for intimacy.

We have found that it is often difficult to engage in the learning process or even connect intimately with all of the noise around. I don't know if your house is like this, but there have been times at our house when we have a TV on in our room, Anthony is playing Guitar Hero in the living room, Ashlyn has a show on in her room, and the dog is barking. Anthony is yelling at Ashlyn; I am yelling at Anthony to leave his sister alone; and then Susie jumps into the picture. It is utter chaos. We all think that we are communicating, but we cannot hear anything for all the noise in our lives. This whole idea of intimacy not only takes self-sacrifice and love but also takes an environment of learning. This environment must be less chaotic.

49

Honestly, we are not the greatest examples of peaceful living. Susie and I often find ourselves in bed watching our TV with the volume turned down. Both of us have our laptops out on our laps tying up late emails or just surfing the web. One night, when I arrived home from a late day at the office, Susie was lying across the bed. The first words out of her mouth were, "It's your turn with Ashlyn. I have had enough!"

Ashlyn was in the bathroom getting ready for bed. When I went in to help her along, she started ranting and raving screaming, "I want momma! I want my mommyyyyyyyyyyy!" " I hate you. I don't like you. You're the meaner!" I took Ashlyn calmly by the face and caught her eyes with mine, which doesn't happen too often. When she caught my eyes, she immediately stopped and gazed up at me and proclaimed, "Daddy! I love you!" Despite all of the chaos going on in her head, when she stopped and really saw me, she responded to me.

How often do we walk right by the ones we love, distracted by all of the chaos in our worlds, and never stop, look into their eyes and truly see them, hear them, and reach the deepest places of their soul? This is intimacy-stopping long enough to connect on a deeper level and finding that familiar closeness again.

I trust that many of you are seeing now that this challenge is far more than the mechanics of intercourse or 30 straight days of sex. You see I am learning a lot about intimacy during this series. I know I knew the meaning, but I think it sometimes gets muddy, especially when sex is involved. So let's take another look at the meaning of intimacy from Dictionary.com:

Intimacy-

1. The state of being intimate.
2. A close, familiar, and usually affectionate or loving personal relationship with another person or group.
3. A close association with or detailed knowledge or deep understanding of a place, subject, period of history, etc.: an intimacy with Japan.

4. An act or expression serving as a token of familiarity, affection, or the like: to allow the intimacy of using first names.
5. An amorously familiar act; liberty.
6. Sexual intercourse.
7. The quality of being comfortable, warm, or familiar: the intimacy of the room.
8. Privacy, esp. as suitable to the telling of a secret: in the intimacy of his studio.[8]

I personally think that the third definition hit the nail on the head. The sad reality is sometimes, as husbands, we do not get what our spouse really needs because we are so consumed with ourselves. We miss looking at the other person or their desires as even being valid. This goes both ways.

Men, it is time to get off of the couch and help your wife with the kids and help clean up around the house.

And women, it is time for you to get rid of those old ratty pajamas, turn up the heat in the bedroom, and start pleasing your husband.

Remember it is all about this Biblical principle of self-sacrifice, which really is simply putting the other person first. Frankly, if we truly love our spouse, should it not be "their way, right away?"

What is the fundamental character of your relationship right now? Does it reflect the following passage of Scripture?

Philippians 2:1-8 (NLT)
[1]Is there any encouragement from belonging to Christ? Any comfort from His love? Any fellowship together in the Spirit? Are your hearts tender and sympathetic? [2]Then make me truly happy by agreeing wholeheartedly with each other, loving one another, and working together with one heart and purpose. [3]Don't be selfish; don't live to make a good impression on others. Be humble, thinking of others as better than yourself. [4]Don't think only about your own affairs, but be interested in others, too, and what they are doing. [5]Your attitude should be the same that Christ Jesus had. [6]Though He was God, He did not demand and cling to His

rights as God. [7]He made himself nothing; He took the humble position of a slave and appeared in human form. [8]And in human form He obediently humbled Himself even further by dying a criminal's death on a cross.

This is the picture of love that Christ has given us to follow. It is the pathway to greater intimacy. His example is about having the attitude of others first. From experience, I can tell you that it is not easy. Even this week has been difficult for Susie and me. The following is an entry from our **30daysexchallenge** journal from yesterday. "Dear Paul, today I felt as if you were harsh with your words. I need more compassion, and I respond better when you are kinder and gentler with me."

Ouch! That hit me right between the eyes! I had to go back and make things right with her so that our intimacy would continue.

If we are keeping "rightness" between us and putting each other first, an amazing environment will be evident and you will begin to experience intimacy much like the following couple:

Song of Songs 2:1-7 (NLT)
"Young Woman:
[1]"I am the rose of Sharon, the lily of the valley."
Young Man:
[2]"Yes, compared to other women, my beloved is like a lily among thorns."
Young Woman:
[3]"And compared to other youths, my lover is like the finest apple tree in the orchard. I am seated in his delightful shade, and his fruit is delicious to eat. [4]He brings me to the banquet hall, so everyone can see how much he loves me. [5]Oh, feed me with your love—your 'raisins' and your 'apples'—for I am utterly lovesick! [6]His left hand is under my head, and his right hand embraces me. [7]"Promise me, O women of Jerusalem, by the swift gazelles and the deer of the wild, not to awaken love until the time is right.

Now that is some pretty hot stuff right there in the Bible. Notice the placement of the young man's left hand under her head and his right hand embrace. An environment of care and security is evident in their relationship, while admiration for her lover is very evident as well. I don't know about you, but I think a relationship of love like that would be pretty amazing.

What kind of environment are you creating in your relationship? Does it revolve around you or are you making sure that you are connecting with God and the person that He has placed in your life? Maybe today you need to change your order. Even if you have been placing the same order for years, isn't it time to decide that it needs to be Christ's way, right away so that you and your spouse can begin putting each other first and ultimately becoming satisfied in your relationship?

Describe the environment of your marriage.

_____

_____

_____

_____

_____

_____

_____

_____

_____

_____

_____

_____

_____

_____

_____

_____

_____

_____

_____

_____

_____

_____

_____

_____

Re-Read Philippians 2:3-4.
What are some practical everyday ways that you can put your spouse first?

_____

_____

_____

_____

_____

_____

_____

_____

_____

_____

_____

_____

_____

_____

_____

_____

"You've Lost That Lovin' Feelin'?"

I can't help remembering that old 70's song, so please indulge me here a moment. "…You've lost that lovin' feeling now it's gone, gone, gone, wooooooh…!"[9]

Strangely enough, we all have lost that lovin' feelin' at one point or another in our relationships. But, even stranger to me is that there are many, who believe, really believe, that, once it is gone, then it has somehow, "poof", vanished forever!

I recall a counseling session not so long ago where the guy in the relationship was cheating on his girlfriend. They came to us for help because they were in their late 20's and had invested a lot of their time and energy into their relationship. He admitted openly that he did not feel love for her anymore and was stunned when I mentioned the idea that he could fall in love with her again if he wanted to. He replied to my statement by saying. "Wow, I didn't know I could rekindle the love that I once had for her. Just how does that work?"

It is work, hard work. One must be willing to attempt to reengage when there has been love lost. The difficult part is figuring out why the love was lost in the first place. In this couple's situation, they had drifted apart, and he was lured away by another woman. Once fully in an unfaithful relationship, of course, the feelings of love transferred to the third party. Otherwise, there wouldn't be a willingness to risk the current relationship and dive into a cheating relationship.

Just how does such transference of love take place?

We believe it all begins to take place in the mind. For most couples, the wayward partner begins thinking about his great dissatisfaction with his current relationship. The reasons may vary - resentment, boredom, unresolved issues, unforgiveness, the attraction of a third party, etc. This battle in the mind is subtle at first. But, when someone else comes along, the idea of cheating becomes fertile soil to "justify" the thoughts that began as simple dissatisfaction. The justification often leads to what we call "emotional shut-down."

When this mind-set is affirmed by our reasoning, we begin to believe that "what" we think about our relationship is accurate even if it isn't. Since the way we feel is almost always based upon what we think, our actions then follow our feelings. We think we are not in love; thus, we feel that we are not in love. We experience "emotional shut-down."

It is even cyclical in nature. Since we have "felt" we are not in love anymore and we have allowed our minds to continually think "I don't love that person anymore," we are dangerously close to acting like we don't love that person anymore. This cycle is so difficult emotionally that many often find the relationship just too costly to put forth the emotional effort.

Although "emotional shut-down" may seem to be the death of a relationship, my supposition to you is: If we can "think" our way to emotional shut-down, we certainly can "think" our way back to emotional intimacy. We have hope! We can reconnect!

The next chapter goes into detail about how what we do is essential to how we think, feel and eventually respond to each other.

Discuss how this concept of "thinking" leads to "feeling" and "feeling" leads to "acting." Write a time when you have experienced this sequential concept in your life.

_____

_____

_____

_____

_____

_____

_____

_____

_____

_____

_____

_____

_____

_____

_____

_____

_____

_____

_____

_____

"You Scratch My back, I'll Scratch Yours!"

Continuing with the premise that what we think has a trickle-down effect upon what we feel and ultimately do, I remember an instance at our previous church, the church that was instrumental in church planting Relevant. A group of ladies approached me and some of the other pastor's wives. They wanted to set up a time so that they could meet with us and simply pray over us. Initially, I felt a little nervous at this request. This was a bit different from a typical prayer meeting where you have your basic prayer list and pray down the list for others. This meeting was specifically for us to be prayed over.

We set up a time and met with these dear ladies. They began praying down the row of pastors' wives, and I was last in the row. It was a really sweet time of prayer as they prayed. But, when they reached me, the first thing out of the leader's mouth was "Pain!" She said, "I feel so much pain in this sister." She went on to pray for me, and it was all good. Yet, in my mind, I have never been able to totally shake those first words out of her mouth, "Pain!"

Indeed, many people would say I have had a fair amount of pain in my life. When I think about that experience during that prayer time, I am swept away to the story of Ruth and Naomi in the Bible. These two women returned to Naomi's hometown, and Naomi renamed herself Mara because she had lost both of her sons and her husband and her countenance was so downcast. The name Mara meant, "I am bitter!" (Ruth 1)

I certainly do not want to be called "Mara!" Or "Pain!" I determined that very day that I would not "think" of myself or the life that God had given me as pain, suffering, bitterness or anything other than "joy!"

You see, I have been around bitter people, and I refuse to let the circumstances around me rob me of the joy that God wants to fill up in my heart, my mind, and my entire life.

As much as possible, I reject any thoughts that are counter to God's purpose for my life. I dwell on things that are good, honest, and true. This practice is yet another Biblical principle. The Bible states, *"Summing it all up, friends, I'd say you'll do best by filling your minds and meditating on things true, noble, reputable, authentic, compelling, gracious—the best, not the worst; the beautiful, not the ugly; things to praise, not things to curse. Put into practice what you learned from me, what you heard and saw and realized. Do that, and God, who makes everything work together, will work you into his most excellent harmonies." Phil. 4:8-9 (MSG)* These things are what I think upon. With this in mind, let us examine how we act and react in our relationships.

I have learned that we respond to those in our lives with endearment or aversion usually by how we are treated by them. We make judgments of whether or not we like or dislike people we come in contact with in this world by their treatment of us.

Even my 9-year old judges others almost every day. He gets upset with his neighborhood friends and comes in declaring that "so and so is not my friend anymore!" Another famous statement, "I'm never playing with them again!"

The next time I turn around he is outside playing with the friends he just denounced. As adults, we don't usually make verbal declarations about people; we just keep our judgments to ourselves. Still, we all have to admit that at one time or another we have met someone that we just didn't like.

On the flip side, the way that we treat others will often determine whether or not others will like or dislike us.

This idea goes along with the saying nearly every mother has passed on to her child, "do unto others as you would have them do unto you." Unfortunately, many of us unconsciously walk through our lives without much regard to "how" we treat others. I believe we chalk much of whether others like or dislike us up to our personalities. We rationalize to ourselves, "that is just who I am".

I am not ignorant of the fact that personality does play a part. Sometimes we justify the way we treat others by convincing ourselves that we can't change the way we are. I know that has been true in my life. I have justified the way that I act by trying to convince myself that I can't help the "way I am." "It is just my M. O.!"

Our emotions play such a huge part in our decision to like or dislike someone. I want to share an example of a couple with whom we discussed the idea of emotional oneness.

This couple lived in a generation where the Christian Living section of the bookstore was null and void.

To their credit, they have made the best out of their relationship without Christian psychologists.

As we dug deep into some of their personal struggles, I remember the wife stated that on their honeymoon she had gotten very emotional over something very menial. I believe they were traveling to Niagara Falls and were hurrying to catch a tourist attraction before it closed. She said that she began crying and her new husband sternly pronounced that, "All my life all my mother did was cry and I won't live like that anymore, so stop crying!." She continued to share with us that, since then, she rarely cried in front of her husband throughout their entire marriage.

Although she admitted that she did feel hurt, she just didn't let anyone see her hurt. Could this emotional control be because of the incident so many years ago? I do not know to what degree this couple is emotionally one, but this story really made me think about what is emotional oneness.

One quality that I believe draws a couple toward emotional oneness is compassion. While we need not cry together as a couple, a great deal of comfort comes from a spouse that is compassionate toward our feelings or difficulties. Another step toward emotional oneness comes when we share a significant emotional experience. I know that I was more emotionally one with my husband at the births of our two children than I have been at any other time in our relationship. The joy and exuberance of bringing life into the world together, along with the immense love that we both shared for the child, was such a huge bonding experience.

Still, this couple's story brought me to examine some of the ways I handle my emotional responses to Paul in my quest for emotional oneness. It was interesting to me that, as I examined my own experiences, I found that I follow much of the emotional patterns that my parents modeled. For the most part, I get verbally loud and angry easily. When I feel sad, upset or blue, I usually stuff my feelings and try to move on.

In assessing the importance of connecting in our emotional relationships, I have to admit that working on sharing my hurts and feelings with Paul is imperative to oneness. Still, I often find myself resorting back to my natural coping mechanisms. Since Paul and I are both very strong personalities, this is one area of our relationship that we constantly have to give attention.

I blame myself more than anyone else, because I need to communicate my feelings by whatever means works in order for change to take place. This process of oneness takes work. It is not easy; yet, the feelings and emotions that our spouse has toward us depend upon this work.

In order to change our patterns of behavior, we must identify and assess our relationships. The reality is that we like and dislike our spouse for the most part by how they make us feel. This leads us to the core of why our emotions play such a huge part in our relationship. While we may like someone who makes us laugh and dislike someone who makes us cry, we rank people based upon how much we like or dislike them. We naturally are drawn to people that make us happy, and we try to spend the least amount of time that we can with those people that make us unhappy. When someone makes us extremely happy much of the time, we often cross from simply "liking" that person to "loving" that person. This falling in love is not so much a mystery as once thought. We have learned that discovering what it is that makes us happy is a major key to keeping the "love alive" in our relationship.

In review, we can learn to make our spouses happy by learning what it is that makes them happy, and evading those behavioral patterns that make them unhappy. We have studied the Biblical principles of putting each other first and keeping our minds focused upon good thoughts. Next let's examine another Biblical principle that will greatly affect our marital relationships.

The Scriptures also substantiate the idea of making each other happy. This Biblical principle is found in the following passages:

I Corinthians 7:32-38(NLT)
[32]In everything you do, I want you to be free from the concerns of this life. An unmarried man can spend his time doing the Lord's work and thinking how to please Him. [33]But a married man can't do that so well. He has to think about his earthly responsibilities and how to please his wife. [34]His interests are divided. In the same way, a woman who is no longer married or has never been married can be more devoted to the Lord in body and in spirit, while the married woman must be concerned about her earthly responsibilities and how to please her husband. [35]I am saying this for your benefit, not to place restrictions on you. I want you to do whatever will help you serve the Lord best, with as few distractions as possible. [36]But if a man thinks he ought to marry his fiancée because he has trouble controlling his passions and time is passing, it is all right; it is not a sin. Let them marry. [37]But if he has decided firmly not to marry and there is no urgency and he can control his passion, he does well not to marry. [38]So the person who marries does well and the person who doesn't marry does even better.

The Apostle Paul seems to be commanding married people to spend a great deal of time pleasing each other in their marriage relationship. The Scripture says that those who are not married are actually doing better. I hope you noticed that much of what Paul is saying here is about putting each other first and pleasing each other. The Greek word for "please" is a-res-ko, which means: to accommodate one's self to the opinions, desires and interests of others.[10]

Aresko is the whole foundation for our study and the personal assessment that you each will be taking at the end of the next chapter, and it is found right here in the New Testament. Another interesting fact here is that it is not a suggestion; it is more of a command.

A practical approach to making sure we are making each other happy or "pleasing" our mate is to not only identify what makes our spouse happy or unhappy, but also, focus our time and attention on these specific findings and doing these things daily. This is how to keep the love alive in our relationship, and how to avoid what kills the love in our relationship.

Discovering and learning will take effort but is imperative in this **30daysexchallenge** journey. This process is the means to getting a more intimate marriage and ultimately a better sex life. Now that should motivate all men to research, unpack, and even answer a few questions. I hope everyone is willing to do whatever it takes to love each other more!

The men are now asking: How do we educate ourselves so that we can get on with the sex challenge? The next chapter will take you through a step-by-step process to identify those things that make you happy and unhappy in your relationship. This is the pathway to the sex, men!

Discuss people that you dislike. Name some things that they have done to make you feel disdain or dislike for them.

_____
_____
_____
_____
_____
_____
_____
_____
_____
_____
_____
_____
_____
_____
_____

List some events that you have shared together that have made you closer emotionally.

_____
_____
_____
_____
_____
_____
_____
_____
_____
_____
_____
_____

Take time to study the passage in I Corinthians 7:33-34.

List some of your opinions, desires, and interests that resonate
with your spouse "pleasing" you.

_____

_____

_____

_____

_____

_____

_____

_____

_____

_____

_____

_____

_____

_____

_____

_____

_____

_____

_____

_____

_____

"All The World's A Stage"

Act 1 "The Honeymoon"

A strange phenomenon occurs when a couple falls in love and they marry. The first few months are great. Then, reality hits. They move into an adjustment period where they wake up and wonder just who the person really is that they married. They begin what we call their "Scripts", and the characters develop in the story of their lives. The first act appropriately is the Honeymoon.

As I have briefly explained, this act is usually filled with fairytales and blissfulness. All faults or failures are simply overlooked, and the honeymoon continues. We look upon these early days with great fondness and, if we are completely honest, we often wonder later what happened to us?

Act 2 "A Night at the Improv"

Act 2 is where we will begin our journey into unpacking/studying the Scripts of our lives.

The second act is filled with improvisation. We learn more about this person with whom we are joined in marriage. Greater still, we learn how they act and react to us and to the circumstances of life. In this stage, the Script is filled with inconsistency. There is genuine care and concern to guard each other's feelings at all costs. As the plot thickens in the relationship, the characters are more clearly developed. This is an important part of the Script because the happy ending to the story depends greatly upon the characters interaction and their ability to be compatible. They should make each other happy more than they make each other unhappy. If one or both are unhappy more than they are happy, the relationship may not seem worth the effort and they stop trying to keep the peace and move to Act 3.

Act 3 "When Back Stage Moves Center Stage" – The Climax

As all stories go, there is usually a climax. This is where the "spotlight" shines on the relationship. In this act, the couple adapts to the relationship or escapes the relationship. Character flaws become apparent, and the couple discovers that adapting is not always all that it is cracked up to be. Often, this is the place of discontentment and complacency.

This is the Act in which the realization of the drift is finally recognized. It can also be dangerously close to emotional shutdown for one or both of the characters. Still, it can also be the character's greatest defining moment. They can make a choice to come back to shore instead of continuing to drift. They can reconnect. They can love each other again.

Once we identify the stage of your script, then you as a couple must make a choice. Will you make the choice to do what it takes to be compatible? Will you chose to reconnect and stop the drift? In order to successfully make the choice to save your relationship, you must be prepared to make a definitive change in your Script. This choice will require action.

You and your spouse are the actors in your Script. As actors, you daily play out your Script. The change that must take place we call the "big transition." The big transition is simply moving from actors playing out the same Script over and over again, to directors - directors who make changes in their script.

Either you can remain the actors of your lives - continuing down a path of "Ground Hog Day" living. Or, you will make the choice to become the directors of your lives.

At some point in your play, for a healthy relationship to grow, the actors must make this big transition. The transition from actors to directors simply must happen.

It is imperative to understand that actors live in a fantasy world. They act like things will get better. Actors act like life isn't so bad. They act like things are as good as they get. All of this acting is a big façade. The answer to this satire is what every couple needs - a career change.

In order to make this career change, they must segue into the big transition!

·············· The Big Transition: ··············
Moving from actors to actively directing your script.

Moving from Actors to Directors takes courage and perseverance. With education and patience, any couple can make the big transition.

The process is as follows:

• Scene A: Study the Characters and Your Set

You and your spouse are the characters in your Script. Decipher how you are wired. Recognize the set on which your script is played.

• Scene B: Identify Your Script.

The dialogue of your Script contains the conflicts, character flaws, and even compatibility that are cyclical in your relationship - those things that make you happy and those things that make you unhappy. Your Script is a great editorial as to what extent you "please" your spouse.

• Scene C: Rehearse for the Grand Finale.

Live every day with the intention of bringing down the house!

Job Description for Directors:

Directors instruct, communicate, motivate, facilitate, consummate, postulate, articulate, and often translate.

Meet the characters:

Mr. Deeds	&	Ms. Feelings
Action	vs.	Attitude
Competition	vs.	Conversation
Sight Stimulated	vs.	Touch Stimulated
Admiration	vs.	Affection
Microwave	vs.	Slow Cooker

Mr. Deed's motto is "Actions speak louder than words!"

Ms. Feeling's motto is "Say what you mean, and mean what you say!" Again, there are two foundational Biblical principles that speak directly to the actions of our characters:

1. Put others before yourself… Philippians 2:4 (NIV)

2. Please your spouse according to the definition in the Greek – A-res-ko "to accommodate one's self to the opinions, desires and interests of others."[11]

I Corinthians 7: 33-34. "…How he may please his wife….how she may please her husband."

Discuss the characteristics of Mr. Deeds and Ms. Feelings and how each of you relates to these characteristics – both your similarities and your differences.

_____

_____

_____

_____

_____

_____

_____

_____

_____

_____
_____
_____
_____
_____
_____
_____
_____
_____
_____
_____
_____
_____
_____
_____
_____
_____
_____

Do the "Script" Assessment in Appendix C.

The Rehearsal

As Directors of your Script, you have the ability to rewrite, edit, and redirect where your story is going. Now, it is time to examine your Script and decide which areas need to be edited, or even cropped out of the script, and those that need a rewrite. You must pinpoint your own character flaws as well as your spouses.

The rehearsal is where we begin to put our spouse first and begin to please him/her by giving preference to their opinions, desires, and interests.

An editor (counselor) may be needed in order to mediate some difficult issues that may be discovered during this stage. Still, the work is just beginning. Revisit every question from your assessments in Appendix C and highlight any area that is ranked 3 or lower.

This exercise will help you identify the conflicts within your Script. It will also help identify those areas of your Script that build love for one another by pleasing your spouse.

Pay particular attention to the areas that are circled "extremely important" yet are marked low. These are the "main ideas" of your Script. These main ideas will be the focus of your **30daysexchallenge**. We encourage you to rehearse these main ideas. The 30 days of questions are directed at aiding in the editing, cropping, and rewriting of your scripts and, ultimately, "rehearsing" your Script.

The goal is that after the **30daysexchallenge** has ended you will both have these practices ingrained into your thinking so that you can easily and effortlessly "please" your spouse on a daily basis.

Make a contract to move from Actors to Directors of your Script. Commit to rehearsing your Script daily by signing in the spaces provided.

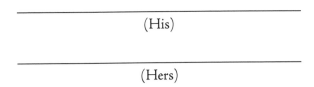

_____

(His)

_____

(Hers)

As a directing team, you may need to implement the 3 C's to conflict resolution in order to begin the process for change found in the latter chapter of the book. What if you are still having difficulty? Follow the story of one of our couples in our **30daysexchallenge** small group.

What if your characters are not compatible? For one of the couples that participated in the challenge, this was the case. When they identified their Script and, specifically, what it was that made them unhappy, they realized that affection was important to both of them. This was easy enough.

The wife noted that it was extremely important to her that her husband be committed to the care and nurture of their children. Since he was a great dad and spent much of his home time playing with their nine month old, she felt pretty happy about their Script. However the "Script" that her husband had developed seemed to cycle around the cleanliness of their home. It wasn't much of a surprise when they discovered that he was displeased by their home setting as she admittedly hates cleaning house.

Not only was it ranked low on his list, he had already carefully and meticulously developed a daily schedule for her to accomplish in order to keep the house clean!

Before understanding the importance of pleasing my husband in practical areas, I would have, in my anger, dropped kicked my husband - and his "to do list" - out on the couch if he had come home with a plan for me to clean for him!

Fortunately, this wife understands the importance of pleasing her husband as well.

But, here is the crux of their problem. She hates, loathes, and despises cleaning. As do I, by the way. She felt as if the whole Scripting thing just wasn't fair! Still, because they were committed to the **30daysexchallenge**, they communicated and were able to work out a great plan by the end of the following week. They shared within our group how they were able to resolve their conflicting Scripts.

She explained that, when she would complete her "to do list" every week, he would reward her with a surprise or an extra dinner out. This may seem like male chauvinism at first; however, they were putting each other first and directing their Script.

The key is they are both very happy about their agreement! I asked her today what she would do if he didn't bring her a gift at the end of the week. She just smiled and exclaimed: "Of course, there will be times that things don't work out the way I want them to." This couple has studied their characters and realized that they are not perfect. They transitioned from simply acting out their Scripts to actively directing their Scripts. They have a great relationship and have learned, earlier than most that love is giving to others unselfishly and unconditionally. I am confident that this couple will continue to grow in their love for each other.

Still, what do you do during the times that your Script is not fluent and you "feel" like you just don't love that person anymore?

This is a problem that we hear nine times out of ten when we do marriage crisis counseling. I admit it is a very hard place to be. During this time, your love is a person-to-person type of love. The Bible calls it "Phileo".

Phileo love is a brotherly love. You may be experiencing emotional shut-down because of your unhappiness. Your spouse is either neglecting your opinions, desires, and interests, or simply oblivious to what it is that makes you happy. In some relationships, one or both spouses are simply acting selfishly. Still, many times the reason for emotional shut-down is an extra-marital relationship. It is imperative to understand that not all extra-marital relationships are sexual. Many extra-marital relationships are emotional. Unfortunately, in our experiences, those that are emotional affairs are much harder to break off than those that are only sexual. Whatever the reason, how you are "feeling" just isn't enough to sustain a marriage.

With our special needs daughter, we give so much emotionally that there are many times that, as cold as it may seem, I just don't "feel" like loving her. That is when the love of God that is in me because of Christ in my life, enables me to love as God loves -unconditionally and sacrificially. This kind of love is Agape love.

God's love for humanity is an Agape love. Agape love enabled Christ to go to the cross. Agape love enables us to love our partners when we don't "feel" like loving them and when they are unlovely in our eyes. Agape love enabled me to forgive and love Paul even in the midst of my pain and suffering. This love is only accessed through a personal relationship with God by accepting Christ's love for us as our savior and experiencing the forgiveness He offers through His death on the cross.

"This is love: not that we loved God, but that He loved us and sent His son as an atoning sacrifice for our sins." I John 4:10 (NIV)

Agape love will enable those of you experiencing emotional shutdown toward your spouse to re-engage, forgive, and love unconditionally once again.

You should now understand your Scripts and the importance of implementing practical ways of becoming intentional about pleasing each other daily.

Without looking back at the complete personal assessment, list one main idea that you will rehearse in the next 2-3 hours:

_____
(His Idea)

_____
(Her Idea)

SEXUAL CHALLENGE

"So What About The SEX?"

As we begin the process of truly forgiving, putting each other first, emotionally pleasing each other, and rehearsing our Scripts, the intimacy level of our relationship should sky-rocket because significant healing is taking place in our hearts, and our emotions follow. Once our emotions are reset – you feel love for your partner again because you believe they really love you – we can act upon those rekindled emotions. When we are close spiritually and emotionally, it just makes sense that we would want to be close sexually.

Paul mentioned that I haven't written enough about the sex. After all, it is the **30daysexchallenge**!

As we approach the last few days of the challenge, I asked him if he was ready to answer the inevitable million dollar question – the one that we knew the media would be asking him in the next few days. We know everyone wants to know: Did we have sex for 30 days straight?

He assured me that he had already been thinking about it, and he was ready to answer the question. I guess, after people get over the sixth grade locker room mindset, the real question they want answered is: How in the world did you get your wife to be intimate for 30 days straight?

I keep thinking about a verse in Proverbs, *"An honest answer is like a kiss on the lips" (Proverbs 24:26 NIV)*

Honestly, for me, it wasn't as hard as I initially thought it might be. In fact, it was quite easy. I have said from the get-go that the challenge would be easier for the women and harder for the men. Most women are used to meeting their husbands' needs for sexual fulfillment. Yet, for many men learning and implementing the idea of a Script in a practical way to please their wives has been and may continue to be the greatest challenge. If you think about it, what woman wouldn't be thrilled to have her man intentionally work hard at their relationship for 30 days straight?

A few things I had known, yet not thought about until recently, became a reality to me over the course of this month.

First, a woman decides long before she goes to bed whether or not she will be intimate with her spouse that night. I can't emphasize enough how much a woman's thoughts and emotions play into her readiness to be intimate with her mate.

Our church's creative team designed billboards to advertise the **30daysexchallenge** series in Tampa. One of the tag lines they were not permitted to use was: "Are you up for it?"

Mentally, I know that I was "up for the challenge" each night. Still, there is not a man alive who can make his woman be up for the challenge. He can't crawl into her head and make her want to have sex with him. Along the same lines, no woman in her right mind would want to have sex with a man that she is not "right" with. If there isn't "rightness" between the two, then the one flesh thing just isn't going to happen!

As I have said from the beginning, the **30daysexchallenge** is so much more than what is obvious.

The second thing that God made me personally aware of: He really does want us to have passion in our marriage.

From a practical standpoint, long before the **30daysexchallenge** was a glimmer in our church's creative team's eyes, I had prayed that God would increase my sexual desire for my husband. For apparent reasons, I didn't even share this with Paul. I simply prayed about it – prayed even when I questioned whether God would do anything to enhance my passion for my husband.

For years, Paul and I have discussed the vast difference between the male and female libido. The subject came up again a few months ago when I felt as if I really didn't want to meet Paul's sexual fulfillment as much as he needed it met. We would laugh about me taking the little pink pill that is now available for women. It became a standing joke. It just seemed to be a "funny" that we would laugh about and then stop talking about for a while. But, I didn't forget about it. My feelings were still very much there. In fact, I often wondered if something was wrong with me physically. I know that men are like "microwaves" and women are "slow cookers". Still, it was something that I questioned often.

One Sunday morning, not too long ago, I was listening to one of my mentors talk about her relationship with her husband of over 25 years. As she explained how they had begun to pray that their love would be like it was when they first started dating, I listened more intently. Their prayers were answered. He renewed the passion of their first love. She went on to tell about their wonderful rekindled love for each other. Her words captivated me as she continued on to say that it is like they are falling in love with each other all over again. Her faith inspired me to pray more earnestly for our relationship. So I did. Of course, I never dreamed that God would answer me with the **30daysexchallenge**!

Another realization occurred to me during the 30 days. In my world, people didn't talk about the pleasures of sex - only the consequences of immoral sex. I know in all of my years of being in church services, I cannot recall a pastor teaching from the Biblical book The Song of Songs! Even though I believe with all of my heart that my parents believe that sex is not just for procreation, nothing in my world ever verbalized that fact. Personally, I agree with the statements made previously in Paul's message: many people have a misunderstanding about sex because their perception is that all churches view the enjoyment of sex as sinful and that sex is for procreation purposes exclusively.

This is one issue where the church seems to have taken a vow of silence and, thus, made talking about it taboo. Meanwhile, the prevailing culture has become more and more outwardly explicit about sex, breeding wrong perceptions that even Christians accept.

The number one question the media has asked me is: "Just what did I think about the challenge when my husband came home and told me about it?"

My answer: I knew it would improve the overall marriage relationship for our church members, because I knew the challenge was far more than just intercourse. I was excited about it.

Again, what woman wouldn't love for her husband to concentrate on working on their relationship for 30 days straight?

But now I realize the results for me, personally, have been even greater than even I had anticipated. In speaking with some of the women in our church, I asked them if they, too, had experienced any change in their libido during the challenge. Amazingly, I was not alone. With the exception of one woman who already experienced sexual fulfillment in her Script, they all agreed that the abundance of sex had a healthy effect on their relationship and increased their desire for sex with their husbands. They seemed as surprised as I was about the results, so I questioned them about the idea that mental preparedness for a female was another key to the success of the **30daysexchallenge.**

Again, they agreed and snickered as they openly admitted that they do decide whether or not they will be intimate with their husbands long before their spouse initiates intimacy.

During our girls discussion, another fact came to light that was an eye-opener for us all: We all agreed that most women only need sex a couple of nights per month to be sexually fulfilled.

We concluded that hormones affected our libidos in the past, but the challenge made us realize the significance of pleasing our spouses on a daily basis! The more we gave, the more they gave.

One of the women mentioned that she believed her sex drive did not necessarily increase but that she felt more "in the mood" because of the increased amount of time that she and her husband spent in conversation before bed.

We were not only shocked when our husbands met their end of the challenge by daily working on our Scripts but were even more surprised that our passion and sexual desire for our husbands increased considerably. We concluded that sexual intimacy would probably not become a daily habit because, honestly, the men were just too tired. However, connecting intimately should and would become a daily goal.

At the end of the 30 days, I had a greater sexual desire for my husband. And, I am certain now, more than ever, that God cares about my personal life, even the most intimate places in my heart. I also know that it is my responsibility to act upon what I know rather than what I feel. I need to be mentally ready, just like an athlete gets mentally prepared, to meet my husband's needs - whatever they may be. As I focus on how I am loved by him, rather than how I am feeling, God will keep my desire at the level that my husband needs it to be. Of course, he must, in return, continue to love me and keep things "right" between us. He must strive to please me and rehearse our Script for our relationship to continue to be successful. Well, that is our goal anyway. Our Scripts take a lot of grace and mercy. Our actions should lead to successfully rehearsing our Scripts and to pleasing each other sacrificially.

List in the following blanks some ways that you know, not simply feel but believe in your mind, that you are loved by your spouse?

_____
_____
_____
_____
_____
_____
_____
_____
_____
_____
_____
_____

When we truly believe that we are loved, our emotions will follow. We have all heard the saying that, "make-up sex is the best sex!" Now we hope you fully understand the reasoning behind that statement.

List why mental preparedness aids a woman in pleasing her husband's sexual desires.

_____

_____

_____

_____

_____

_____

_____

_____

_____

_____

_____

_____

_____

Discuss why you believe that God intends sexual relations to be enjoyable within marriage? If you do not agree, discuss with your mate your beliefs.

_____

_____

_____

_____

_____

_____

_____

_____

_____

_____

_____

_____

Sex Is Sacred!

Oh, we didn't really want to think that sex is sacred. That thought destroys all of the times that we may have thought about sex outside of marriage. It makes justifying pornography difficult and our "oh so private" thought life. So, why is this Biblical principle of sacred sex so important?

For one, we believe that our current culture, as with past cultures, has twisted and perverted what God created to be beautiful and pleasurable within the covenant of marriage.

Sex is the most intimate act that a couple can share and that is a fact that almost everyone can agree upon.

I do want to clarify what we believe the Bible teaches about the marriage bed.

The Bible says, *"Marriage is honorable and the marriage bed is pure." Hebrews 13:4 (NIV)*

This is referring to keeping unfaithfulness out of a marriage. We believe that all sexual activity is pure before God within the covenant of marriage, whatever that may mean for you as a married couple.

The Song of Songs (a book from the Bible) is an explicit and beautiful picture of sexual acts within the marriage bed. However, everything must be done with mutual agreement and respect between both spouses. Marriage is honorable, and we honor each other within it. This is a key principle to live by. True love would never demand something from the one it loves.

Because of my religious upbringing, I believed that there were strict guidelines of do's and don'ts, and that the porn industry had just warped most male thinking so that they believed that sex is like a pornographic movie. I still believe that some of our thinking about sex, both male and female, is not God's thinking about sex. Perverted sex is never God's idea of sex. Bringing pornography into your relationship, even when viewed together, defiles God's plan of oneness and unity between the two of you in the covenant of marriage.

Remember when you stood at the altar before God. It wasn't you two and the porn star making vows to each other on the day you were married. I know many have bought into the lie that pornography makes the marriage bed creative. I believe that God is more creative than the porn industry, and He has given us great imaginations and creativity. After all, we are made in His image. He is too creative to just give us one boring, redundant position.

Describe how you feel about the sacredness of the marriage bed and your thoughts about pornography within marriage. You may also want to discuss how your parents viewed sexual activity and the atmosphere in which you were raised.

_____
_____
_____
_____
_____
_____
_____
_____
_____
_____
_____
_____

PHYSICAL CHALLENGE

Each couple will encounter bad reviews in their relationship. We will neglect or even forget what we have studied and encountered over the course of the last 30 days. We may even put our needs before our spouses. We will have bad performances! So how do we physically endure or create stamina for the long run of our marriages? Just like an athlete prepares for a triathlon, we must physically be in shape for our relationships to endure.

In the next four chapters we have intentionally targeted specific areas in our relationships that, when healthy, will aid in creating stamina and aid in avoiding the "bad reviews" in our scripts.
They are:

> How to build a harmonious environment,
> How to resolve conflicts,
> How to forgive yourself, and
> How to build communication for 30 days.

Creating an Ethos

For the **30daysexchallenge** to be successful in your marriage, the spiritual, emotional, and sexual all need to be right in your relationship. Let's explore how to build a harmonious environment of love in which each challenge can not only be met, but also maintained, in your relationship.

Harmony in the intimate places of your relationship will reflect the success of your challenge. We have found that couples need a standard or system in which to measure frequently the temperature of their relationship.

This standard is much easier grasped when visualized as a gathering place. This place is called our "Ethos."

Ethos, according to The Oxford English Dictionary, is defined as "the characteristic spirit, prevalent tone of sentiment, of a people or community; the 'genius' of an institution or system." However, the word ethos has been translated to contain many different meanings within the English language. One such definition is that the concept of ethos adheres to accepted standards, rather than what is more modernly thought of as character unique to a certain individual. S. Michael Halloran states in his research that "the most concrete meaning given for the term in the Greek lexicon is 'a habitual gathering place.'"[12]

To clarify, his reference to the meaning of ethos as a habitual gathering place draws more attention to an inferred, rather than a literal, meaning. In a place where one might gather often, the opportunity for developing communal values indefinitely arises. These types of values are those which are established in the meaning of ethos.

Therefore, to be a good example of ethos one must portray the types of traits that are most valued within a society. For example, virtues valued in ancient Athenian society would be "justice, courage, temperance, magnificence, magnanimity, liberality, gentleness, prudence, (and) wisdom."[13]

Creating an Ethos or environment based upon forgiveness, reconciliation, self-sacrifice, and unconditional love - God's Checed love in the Hebrew; or God's Agape love in the Greek - is our goal. It is where our beliefs about God and the Bible are in harmony with our practices and customs about ourselves and how we treat others, especially those we claim to love.

Frequently returning to our "Ethos" and measuring our relationship will promote the stamina in which we are striving. Maintaining stamina is vital because as our environment/ethos is harmonious then our intimacy level is off the charts; and, if sex is one of the main ideas in our Script, then it, too, will be off the charts.

The down side to all of this is, when any of the three intimacies (spiritual, emotional, or sexual) are not functioning harmoniously, our "Ethos" is disrupted. There is an immediate need to return to our "gathering place", so that we can establish harmony again based upon the virtues we value as a couple. And, beware: In any typical relationship, on any given day, our "ethos" can, and probably will, be disrupted.
The key point is to return to the first mini-challenge: Spiritual Challenge. After identifying the problem, forgive again. We are imperfect people and live in an imperfect world. As the Bible teaches us, we have to *"...forgive, just as God through Christ has forgiven you." Phil. 4:32b (NIV)*

Sometimes that may mean daily work before you can meet the emotional and physical needs of your spouse.

Another way to look at our Ethos is to compare it to a report card. Our children are monitored frequently in order to make sure that they are "making the grade." If they are not up to grade level, their teachers send home progress reports indicating their need for improvement. Thus, as we rehearse our scripts, we must re-turn to our "gathering place"- our Ethos- and grade ourselves. Ask yourselves some complicated questions: Are we meeting the challenges? Does our Script need an assessment review? Are we living out what we have determined as our values as a couple? Imagine how disheartened a parent feels when a child brings home an "F" on a report card when they had no clue that their child was failing the nine weeks. If we do not frequently monitor our relationships, we are in danger not only of a drift in our relationship but also a possible failure as well.

Finally, we hope it is clear that our **30daysexchallenge** is more than just intercourse and that each couple is committed to all four mini-challenges within the **30daysexchallenge**.

Identify and list the core values of your "Ethos" as a couple.

_____

_____

_____

_____

_____

_____

_____

_____

_____

_____

_____

_____

_____

_____

_____

As humans we get busy and forget that we need to return to our Ethos- our gathering place, and grade our relationship. List 2 ways that will remind you to return to make sure your Ethos/Environment is harmonious. (Examples: The first of every month, anniversary dates, calendar an appointment, use a cue word or phrase, or even use the first few minutes of date night each week.)

_____

_____

_____

_____

_____

_____

_____

_____

_____

_____

_____

_____

_____

_____

_____

_____

_____

_____

_____

_____

_____

Conflict Resolution – The Three C's

As I mentioned previously, when things are not right between you and your spouse, this distance can become dangerous and lead to a drift in the marriage. I know that when Paul and I have an argument in the morning, we usually rush our separate ways before we are able to resolve the conflict. For me, I just can't stand it when there is "stuff" between us. When our "rightness" is wrong, my day is completely off! I usually can't focus on anything other than the conflict and what he said and what I said. Not only am I off mentally, but I'm off emotionally and spiritually. I carry the negative emotions with me until we get together and make things right between us again. We know we are not perfect and neither is anyone else. Since conflicts are inevitable in marriage, we have put together some practical steps in helping prevent, diffuse and resolve conflicts.

Our first "C" in resolving conflict is to be calm

Set a time and place that is free from irrational behavior and emotional reactions. When conflict arises in any relationship, it is usually due to a disagreement between the parties. We try to get our way while our partner is trying to get their way. We usually use varied methods to "get our way". Our methods are mostly unhealthy and expressed in the heat of the moment. These unhealthy methods can vary anywhere from irrational behaviors, to passive aggressive behaviors. Most people can identify how they "get their way" very easily. Whatever method you and your spouse use, the conflict is heightened by our emotional connection to "getting our way."

If your current methods of conflict resolution are not working, we have a plan that we pray will be helpful.

First, we want to identify what method you currently use to get your way and to what level you allow yourself to be emotionally connected to the conflicts.

Those that are extremely irrational, who get loud and anger easily, are just as susceptible to losing the love of their spouse during conflicts as those who simply stuff their emotions inside and deny any conflict. Then, there are those that are peace-makers at any cost. They are the diplomats and can sometimes be labeled manipulators. Since each "emotional method" causes loss of love from a spouse, identifying your emotional method of responding to conflict is vitally important in any relationship.

We all face conflicting issues in our Scripts. If we can understand how we act and react and remove the emotions from a sometimes volatile environment to a safe place, we have a much better opportunity to resolve our conflicting issues without losing feelings of love for our spouse.

Take time to identify your methods of getting your way.

_____

_____

_____

_____

_____

_____

_____

_____

_____

_____

_____

_____

_____

_____

It is imperative that you are able to identify this part of your Script quickly and diffuse the emotional connections so that you can implement our next step.

"Stop, Drop, And Roll!"

Back in the mid-1970's, there was a very popular fire safety slogan that some may remember. It was "Stop! Drop! And Roll!"[14] In order to extinguish a fire on yourself you were instructed to Stop, Drop, and Roll! When a heated issue arises in your Script, do the following:

1. Stop the conflict at the conversation level.
2. Drop the subject completely.
3. Roll on to another time and place. Revisit the issue when your emotions are back in balance.

Our second "C" in resolving conflicts is to be creative.

A very popular method to creatively solve problems is to brainstorm. Brainstorming can be fun, and it is a safe means to accomplish what emotional conflict cannot. While you can use a whiteboard, markers, or sticky notes to jot down your ideas while brainstorming, the back of an envelope works just as well. In other words, this is a low-maintenance, low-cost technique. Use these guidelines for your brainstorming sessions.

1. Think out of the box
2. Write every idea down
3. Agree to the solutions whole-heartedly

The Third "C" is to create a contract.

Since we've learned that our "Scripts" are cyclical in our relationships, we can forego many repetitive conflicts by diffusing them before they arise.

As a couple, you must create a contract for resolving conflicts within your marriage. This contract must be entered into by both parties whole-heartedly. The Bible says, *"...make me truly happy by agreeing whole-heartedly with each other, loving one another, and working together with one mind and purpose." Phil. 2:2 (NLT)*

Agreement by both the husband and wife is critical. If you cannot whole-heartedly agree on your conflict resolution techniques when you are calm, the contract will be useless in the heat of an argument.

When a conflict arises, you simply go back to the contract and follow the plan that you have already designed.

Family contracts are especially effective with children old enough to be involved in the creative method.

The child has the opportunity to see the conflict outside of the emotional connection (the heat of the moment) and can choose the consequences ahead of time for their potential behavior. When an issue arises, the parent simply resorts back to the contract that the child helped create and whole-heartedly agreed upon, and the parent has no need to do anything but follow through on the consequences that the child set for himself/herself. A behavior contract may seem, on the surface, quite juvenile for adults. However, think of how juvenile you act and react to one another in the "heat of the moment" when you are both emotionally trying to get your way. Implementing the Three C's in your relationship will keep feelings of love at the right levels. In the space provided, try to resolve a conflict in your "Script" by using the three C's to conflict resolution.

Be Calm!

Find a setting in which you can be calm and collected about your issue If not now, possibly later in the bath tub! No one can be angry if they are naked and vulnerable in the tub together. Write down the issue.

_____

_____

_____

_____

_____

_____

_____
_____
_____
_____
_____
_____
_____

Be Creative!

Creatively brainstorm by using the space below to come up with "out of the box solutions" No bad ideas!

_____
_____
_____
_____
_____
_____
_____
_____
_____
_____
_____

Build A Contract!

Write a contract that you both are whole-heartedly in agreement upon.

_____
_____
_____
_____
_____
_____
_____
_____
_____

For Paul and me, a recurring conflict in our marriage was the fact that our special needs daughter got up very early in the morning. We would both be angry with each other when we felt that the other one wasn't pulling his/her fair weight in taking care of her morning routine. A former pastor suggested to us that we take turns and set days that we each would get up and help her get ready for the day. This contract has been effective for us for over six years. I no longer lay in bed feeling guilty that I made Paul get up, and, when my day rolls around, I simply know it is my turn. I don't get upset or carry feelings of resentment toward Paul. I believe even the little conflicts that go unaddressed play big on our emotions. They build walls of resentment which, if unaddressed, can easily turn into feelings of bitterness in a relationship. Obviously, these issues can easily become a bad part of our Script if they go on and on without resolution.

In the following space, take time to write down any unresolved issues that you have been sucking up inside in order to keep the peace. Also set a time to use the three C's to resolve these unaddressed issues within your Script.

_____

_____

_____

_____

_____

_____

_____

_____

_____

_____

_____

_____

_____

_____

_____

_____

_____

_____

_____

_____

_____

_____

_____

_____

_____

Conflict resolution is rarely a pretty picture, yet implementing these steps, we pray, will help you both keep the feelings of love for each other strong. When you practice these steps, you are saying that you want to protect the love that you have and not allow anything to come between you. This statement is a great way to keep your "ethos" in harmony!

Contracts are intended to make everyone satisfied. Remember the definition of a contract is a pre-established resolution that makes everyone happy.

If negotiating doesn't help, and you are wondering how to get help, we have listed some additional books, websites, and counselors at **30daysexchallenge**.com.

God's plan for your marriage is reconciliation and restoration. It can be better than ever if you just give God a chance!

Conscience Monsters – How To Forgive Yourself

During the interviews for this book and in many casual conversations, I came into contact with some very dear people that just seemed to be downcast over their pasts. They grasp the sex challenge, and they totally see the benefits and greatness of doing sex God's way. Still, they expressed deep regrets over their past relationships, even as they admitted that they understood they were forgiven. Their pasts seemed to haunt them like a conscience monster!

If I have ever experienced a glimpse of God's heart, it is evident in the Biblical principle of forgiveness. What these dear friends of mine are struggling with is not that God forgives them, but that they can't forgive themselves. If we are ever going to be completely one with our spouses, we have to be able to get rid of our haunting pasts. While we often live with consequences from our pasts, God's heart is never for us to live under condemnation from our pasts. He sent His Son so that we would be free from our sins, not in bondage to our sins.

Living with regret and living under condemnation from our past is not freedom.

We believe the source of this bondage, at the core, is beguilement. We are deceived by our adversary, the Devil, when we don't take on God's full forgiveness, which includes forgiving yourself. We usually have no problem forgiving others when they come to us broken and sorry. We have learned to "forgive others, even as we have been forgiven." Still, when it comes to forgiving ourselves, many of us find it difficult to let go.

I believe we struggle with forgiving ourselves for several reasons. One may be like the woman who just felt like she had a "debt" to pay, so she carried the past on her shoulders like a heavy cross. She was justifying her unforgiveness towards herself as penance.

What she was really saying by this deception is that Christ's death upon the cross really wasn't enough to cover her sins. She believed that she had to work off the debt herself. This mindset is so counter to the gospel. The Bible says, *"For it is by grace you have been saved, through faith-and this not from yourselves, it is the gift of God-not by works, so that no one can boast." Eph. 2:8-9 (NIV)*

This verse teaches us we cannot earn forgiveness. Christ paid it all on the cross.

Our faith is sealed by faith and faith alone. Nothing we do or don't do can make up the difference. When we live in this deception, we are really living in unbelief. It is the unbelief that Christ just isn't enough.

Another reason one may not be able to forgive himself/herself is the fact that they don't recognize the power of the mind. As we have previously learned, much of what we do begins in our minds. If we allow our minds to dwell on our pasts, this often prohibits us from living in our present. God so wants us to live our lives for Him today. Wouldn't a better use of our pasts be helping those in our present to avoid going through the pain and guilt we have experienced in our pasts? If you are struggling with forgiving yourself for those things that haunt your conscience, and you have already asked God to forgive you, then re-write the following verse in the spaces below.

"He has removed our sins as far from us as the east is from the west." Psalm 103:12 (NLT)

_____

_____

_____

_____

List: Why is Christ's death on the cross enough to cover the sins of your past?

_____
_____
_____
_____
_____
_____
_____
_____
_____
_____
_____
_____
_____
_____
_____
_____
_____
_____
_____
_____
_____
_____
_____
_____
_____
_____

Communicate!

In conclusion, we have learned that each challenge in the program will need to be clearly communicated in order to achieve the goals of the **30daysexchallenge.** We have offered spaces to communicate with your partner through journaling. We hope this has been a benefit for you and your spouse. After completing the reading and discussion questions at the end of the chapters, you should be well equipped for making your **30daysexchallenge** a success.

Many people have discovered that the **30daysexchallenge** journal was helpful in starting to open the lines of communication. It was amazing to interview couples who used the journal. We found that some actually wrote out their thoughts. Exchanging the journal sometime throughout the day was helpful to some. Others simply found the questions prompted healthy discussions. For many of these couples, just talking was beneficial. The idea, of course, is to keep communication going. The first edition of the **30daysexchallenge** guide can be found at blog.relevantchurch.com.

Paul and I have developed new questions for your 30 days that we hope will encourage you to keep the communication flowing. They are located in Appendix A. Read the Scriptures and discuss the questions or journal back and forth in the space provided. Make every effort to be intimate - spiritually, emotionally, and physically - for the entire 30 days. Because of the nature of some of the questions, some couples may find that being sexually intimate every day is difficult because of unresolved issues, conflicts and adjusting to their Scripts. Remember this exercise is a 30-day rehearsal for the grand finale. Not all rehearsals are great. Some rehearsals will be better than others. When considering giving up, keep in mind: "the show must go on!"

Break a leg!!!

Appendix A
30DaySexChallenge
Questions and Journaling Guide

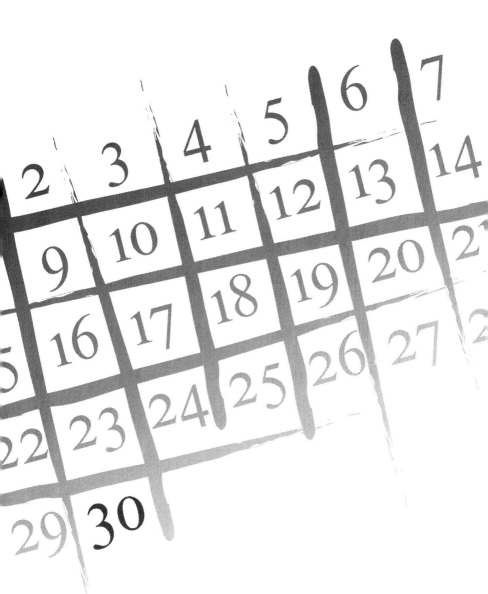

Day 1:

Proverbs 24:26

What areas of the book have posed questions about your relationship? Discuss or journal your thoughts.

Rate on a scale from 1-5 how easy or difficult it is for you to talk openly about sex.

Day 2:

Proverbs 1:7

What is it that each of you hope to gain from this study? In reading the book, have your expectations about the 30day-sexchallenge changed? Why or why not?

Talk about your first sexual encounter and how that experience has affected your sexual relationships.

JOURNAL:

_____
_____
_____
_____
_____
_____
_____
_____
_____

JOURNAL:

_____
_____
_____
_____
_____
_____
_____
_____
_____
_____
_____
_____
_____
_____
_____
_____
_____
_____
_____
_____
_____
_____
_____
_____
_____
_____
_____

Day 3:

Proverbs 13:12

What are your spouse's main ideas from his/her Script? If this is your second set of 30-day questions, repeat back to your spouse one way to practically please them.

An example: By making love to you, I am pleasing you and effectively rehearsing our Script. Or, by taking time to stop and look into your eyes and ask about your day when I get home, I am pleasing you and rehearsing the main ideas of affection and conversation.

Tonight take the time to talk intimately about those things that please you the most sexually.

Day 4:

Colossians 3:13

The first step in most relationships, after discovering your main ideas from your script, will be a time of confession and forgiveness. Each of us fails each other multiple times a day. If this is the first or second set of 30 day questions, a good dose of honest confession and forgiveness is usually in order. Start by saying "I am wrong for not ...... or I am sorry for......."

Practice make up sex!

Day 5:

Ephesians 4:25-27

List anything that is a "cause" for not wanting to please your spouse and rehearse these main ideas. Journal or discuss how this makes you feel and keep in mind to stop drop and roll if the old Script emerges.

Take a long bath together while discussing your answers.

Day 6:

Song of Songs 1:2-2:7.

Reminisce about your first meeting.

If yesterday's rehearsal was difficult, then today try to brainstorm ways that will make pleasing each other a joy rather than a daunting task.

JOURNAL:

Day 7:

Proverbs 5:18

Make up a poem that has a theme of one of your spouse's main ideas. It can be humorous or even romantic. Leave the poem in a special place where your spouse can find it easily.

Think of a more erotic way to express your poem to each other.

Day 8:

Romans 12:10

List some reasons why rehearsing your main ideas on a daily basis is difficult or easy.

Brainstorm a creative way to please your spouse sexually.

JOURNAL:

JOURNAL:

Day 9:

Proverbs 16:3

List creative, "out of the box" ways to make pleasing your spouse easier. Be specific acording to your main ideas.

Express how many times per week that you would like to have your sexual needs fulfilled.

Day 10:

Proverbs 13:20

How has this program affected others around you, especially in regards to your children? Journal your thoughts and feelings.

Practice a new form of foreplay tonight.

JOURNAL:

JOURNAL:

Day 11:

Proverbs 12:17-19

If there is anything that you are keeping to yourself and not willing to open up with your spouse, ask yourself why. Consider a plan and time period in which to reveal what is still hidden. If journaling, let your spouse know by saying something like, "I feel afraid because of what your reaction may be to what I keep hidden in my heart from you. Reassuring me of your commitment to placing safety first in our relationship will help me feel secure in sharing the hidden parts of me.

Day 12:

Proverbs 10:12

What progress, if any, has been made in your relationship? If you are still working on the "forgiveness side of love, then assure your spouse today of your commitment to see this difficult time through." Lighten up with a romantic movie together.

Say a line to your spouse from the movie before making love.

Day 13:

Proverbs 25:11

Write down at least one positive statement about all that you have been uncovering, and thank your spouse for being patient with you.

Honestly discuss how making love for 13 days straight has affected your relationship.

Day 14:

Proverbs 15:22

Halfway through, determine how you are doing on a scale of 1 – 10. Discuss if you have a legitimate need to seek an outside counselor or person that you both respect and love such as a pastor or wise couple.

Give your spouse a massage tonight

JOURNAL:

JOURNAL:

Day 15:

Proverbs 5:19

Describe to your spouse your dream date.

Set a time to fulfill some or part of the date.

Day 16:

Song of Songs 2:8-3:5

Discuss what place spiritual intimacy may have in your relationship.

Day 17:

Proverbs 12:25

Make a reminder on a piece of paper, note card, or sticky note that tells your spouse how much you are looking forward to being intimate (whatever that looks like to you as a couple) tonight.

Day 18:

Proverbs 15:23

Make up a "cue" word or phrase that humorously reminds your spouse when your Script is bad, and a rehearsal is needed. If your sexual intimacy is not good, communicate the need for improvement in a kind manner.

JOURNAL:

JOURNAL:

Day 19:

Proverbs 21:21

Buy or make a tangible item that you can place somewhere in your home as a reminder of the challenge and all the effort that you are making during this 30 days.

Day 20:

Song of Songs 3:6-5:1

Make a cue for your spouse that lets them know that all is well with you and the home. A few examples are: candles burning when they arrive home would cue them that all is well, or a red magnet on the refrigerator means I need a hug.

JOURNAL:

JOURNAL:

Day 21:

John 15:12

What are some more creative ways that you can express to your spouse what it looks like to please you referring to your main ideas. Now think about this in regard to your sexual relationship.

Day 22:

Proverbs 18:16

Send your spouse a surprise.

JOURNAL:

Day 23:

Proverbs 17:9

Ask your spouse if there is anything that they can think of that needs forgiven? Forgive it.

Day 24:

Psalm 20:4

What action steps do you need to take now, to assure each other that you will continue to communicate regularly in your marriage? Some ideas are as follows: additional couple's books, developing your own set of 30 day questions, going to a couples retreat together.

JOURNAL:

JOURNAL:

Day 25:

Proverbs 4:25-26

Write out a plan that is mutually acceptable to each of you that will keep you accountable to work on being intimate with each other for the future of your marriage.

Day 26:

Proverbs 12:4

What parts of the challenge or questions were the most difficult for each of you? Explain why.

JOURNAL:

JOURNAL:

Day 27:

Proverbs 15:21

Are there still adjustments that need to be made? How confident are you that the main ideas of your Script are accurate? If adjustments need to be made, share your commitment to one another that you will do whatever it takes to get this right.

Day 28:

James 1:2-4; Proverbs 16:23-24

Use your best communication style to write a letter of appreciation to your spouse for seeing the challenge and the questions to the end.

JOURNAL:

JOURNAL:

Day 29:

Ecclesiastes 4:9-12

Renew your commitment to each other. Express this renewal verbally. Buy a piece of jewelry or even a temporary tattoo (found in the children's toy sections) to express your love for your spouse.

Day 30:

I Corinthians 13

Make a date to celebrate your achievements and successes from the month!

JOURNAL:

JOURNAL:

Please email us a brief description of your challenge. We are so for you and know that God is for you!

May God bless you and keep you. May He lift up His face upon you and give you peace.

**Sincerely,
Paul and Susie Wirth**

For additional information please visit us online at www.30daysexchallenge.com

Appendix B

RESULTS FROM THE

30DAYSEXCHALLENGE.COM

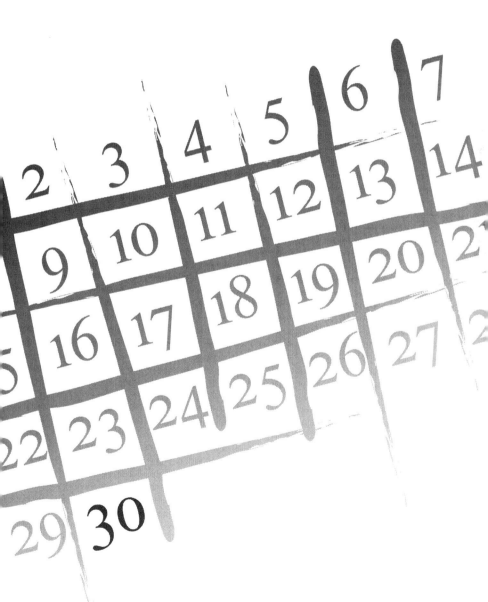

This anonymous survey was taken by participants at the end of their **30daychallenge.** It was offered online at blog.relevantchurch.com; and at Relevant Church during church services the last week of the **30daysexchallenge** message series.

In the week following the challenge, approximately 540 people participated. The results are compiled below.

A large percentage was people participating in the challenge via the internet and downloading the guides. We still receive several emails a day of people asking for the downloadable guides and information.

This great cry for help has greatly motivated us to write this book.

Over 50% of those surveyed were between the ages of 20-39. Approximately 25% were in their 40's

The gender lines were split down the middle.

In response to the question, "Do you think that your relationship has improved over the course of the challenge? 91.3% responded yes.

In response to the question, "What area of your relationship improved the most?"
- Communication – 25.7%
- Emotional connection – 15.7%
- Sex life – 14.3%
- Greater focus on relationship – 38.6%
- Other – 16%

The following are quotes that were provided in the "Additional Comments" section of the original survey.

"It revolutionized my husband and my relationship. We are even thinking about taking the emotional needs test and the 30daysexchallenge every 5 years (same dates since our anniversary is on March 17th). We know our needs will change over time and think it will be great to continue on."

"It was a very freeing few days. At first I wasn't sure where I was going to fit in, BUT in the end I was totally blown away by what it brought out in me."

"AMAZING series! I want to do it again with more time to focus on it daily!"

"I am not sure if there is a post challenge to the 30daysexchallenge, but I have to say that I would be very interested. Thanks for being a forward thinking religious entity."

"We absolutely loved the journaling that we were able to do with one another every day; that will be one of the things that we have decided will be a part of our daily experience in loving and serving one another. It was a great place to connect and share intimate feelings. Thanks again for being bold and courageous for the sake of the relationships in Tampa and beyond."

"I learned from this survey that he doesn't like when I say bad things about myself like 'I'm fat' or I'm ugly', and he also feels like I don't always listen to him so I've been very intentional about working on those things."

"I was able to share this with co-workers and before day two I had three wives who asked me for questionnaires and booklets. These women circled me at work and I believe made me want this more than ever before and I felt accountable to them. I almost felt like their personal cheerleader! Every day I was able to stay strong knowing that I was not in this alone.

"The challenge came at a perfect time in our lives. Our world would be a better place if we were more relaxed, rested (sex offers that) and connected with our spouse. Thanks again for offering this awesome study."

"This was a great idea. Thank you for the thoughtfulness you shared with the whole world!"

"Thanks for this challenge. I heard about it on TV and the radio. It has greatly improved my marriage and brought back the romance."

"Our life has been extremely rough, and to see another couple go through the same things in life and still pull through that is what true love and commitment is all about."

"I'm so glad that I learned her emotional needs now, before we're married. It's like having the playbook for the other team or the answers for the test you're about to take. Thanks to God and to Relevant for giving us some great tools for our relationship."

"What was so remarkable for me is the way that our lives have changed as a result of saying "Okay so we are going to have sex everyday". We had to make that work for us which meant turning off the TV, talking with a bottle of wine, putting our relationship over our children. I feel like a different person."

"This has been a very beneficial month in the relationship of my wife and me."

"What better way to PREVENT divorce statistics than to cover the two most vital issues back to back. Others can get offended, but our relationships will reflect the Truth."

"This study helped us not only learn new things about each other, but also bring to light those minor adjustments that we could make, that with God's help will help our marriage last a lifetime."

"I think, even though it was difficult for us, that this 30-day challenge is extremely needful and useful, particularly in the church. I think if Christians realize that it is invented by God and is to be enjoyed; that couples would talk about it more and work on it, as well as their relationship needs more often."

"Great overall."

"Wonderful communication tool."

"This series has been the best, most thought-provoking approach I've ever heard on the subject."

Some have asked how we are doing in our relationship the last 10 years since we have studied and taken our marriage relationship head-on. A list of accomplishments, and successes could be compiled for outward appearance sake. While our life together has been greatly fulfilling and a journey of faith, quite frankly, we have had many ups and downs. We are in no way perfect and want to relieve everyone else of that aspiration as well. In fact, we stumbled into the trap of our old Script tonight. My afternoon went downhill dealing with Ashlyn's toilet-training. Anthony was asleep, and I just curled up in bed and wished the world away. But, the world didn't go away, and Paul came home to a frazzled setting with no dinner ready and we expected company to arrive within the hour. Our atmosphere was slightly heated until we both realized that we needed to stop, drop, and roll. We scurried around getting ready for the company, took Anthony to ball practice, and ended the evening with store-bought sushi. We fall prey to our old Script, and it plays us.

If only life was like our four-night vacation last month. No problems, just paradise. It was Costa Rica. I had to stop and look Paul in the eyes as we walked along the shore. I told him to remember how great we are together because sometimes we lose sight of our love for one another when life creeps in and steals our relationship. We constantly prioritize and reprioritize. But isn't that what we are supposed to do? We fall down, and we get up again. We love each other, we are selfish, we forgive, and we love again. Maybe this is not what is expected from us or even the norm for those who counsel others in marriage to not have it all together yet, we just cannot paint a perfect picture with imperfect people. So, for the most part...we love. I just thought of another title for the book. How about, "I Never Promised You A Rose Garden." Or, have you heard of the classic, "Great Expectations?" What about "Grim Expectations?" Ok, our marriage relationship is a lot better than I am making it out to be, but I do want to be totally honest and sincere when I say marriage is hard work for all of us. Yes, your pastor and his wife are not perfect either! They have to work just as hard as anyone else at making their marriage great. So let us all keep loving and pleasing our spouses.

Appendix C
"Script" Assessment

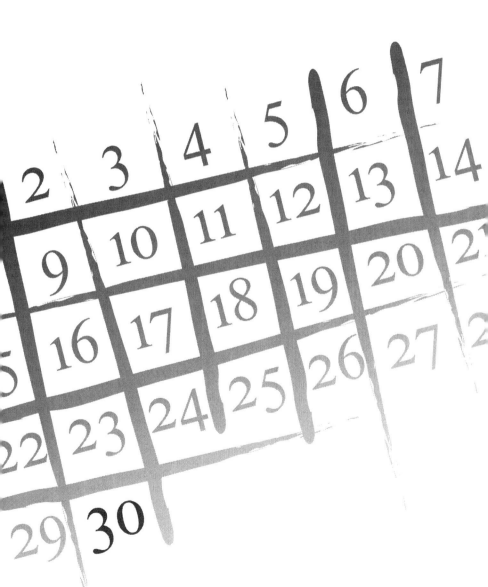

The Key To Identifying Your Script:

Identify your script by examining these areas ranking them 1 as the lowest level of pleasure and 5 bringing the greatest level of pleasure.

Home:

Are you pleased with your home setting?

Cleanliness:

1   2   3   4   5

Clutter:

1   2   3   4   5

Comfort and Décor:

1   2   3   4   5

Peace and Serenity:

1   2   3   4   5

Kids:

Are you pleased with your family setting?

Educational Guidance:

1   2   3   4   5

Moral/Spiritual Guidance:

1   2   3   4   5

Nurture/Care/Discipline:

1   2   3   4   5

Financial Portfolio

Are you pleased with your family's financial setting?

Income Level:

1	2	3	4	5

Spending Habits:

1	2	3	4	5

Saving & Investing Habits:

1	2	3	4	5

Living on a Budget:

1	2	3	4	5

Character Personalities:

First underline the level of importance each character trait is to you. Second, go back through this section again and circle the level at which you are pleased by your spouse with regard to that trait.

Admiration:

Least important   somewhat important   extremely important

1	2	3	4	5

Affection:

Least important   somewhat important   extremely important

1	2	3	4	5

Trust:

Least important   somewhat important   extremely important

1	2	3	4	5

Authenticity:

Least important   somewhat important   extremely important

1   2   3   4   5

Security:

Least important   somewhat important   extremely important

1   2   3   4   5

Conversational:

Least important   somewhat important   extremely important

1   2   3   4   5

Care, Concern, and Compassion:

Least important   somewhat important   extremely important

1   2   3   4   5

Consistency and Follow–through:

Least important   somewhat important   extremely important

1   2   3   4   5

Spirituality:

Least important   somewhat important   extremely important

1   2   3   4   5

Respect:

Least important   somewhat important   extremely important

1   2   3   4   5

Worth and Value:

Least important   somewhat important   extremely important

1   2   3   4   5

Gentleness:

Least important   somewhat important   extremely important

1   2   3   4   5

Patience:

Least important   somewhat important   extremely important

1   2   3   4   5

Self-control:

Least important   somewhat important   extremely important

1   2   3   4   5

Faithfulness:

Least important   somewhat important   extremely important

1   2   3   4   5

Sexually:

Circle the level at which you are pleased with your spouse in each of the following areas:

Times per/ week:

Least pleased		somewhat pleased		extremely pleased
1	2	3	4	5

Foreplay activities:

Least pleased		somewhat pleased		extremely pleased
1	2	3	4	5

Sharing fantasies about each other:

Least pleased		somewhat pleased		extremely pleased
1	2	3	4	5

Visually stimulated:

Least pleased		somewhat pleased		extremely pleased
1	2	3	4	5

Openly sharing sexual expectations and pleasures:

Least pleased		somewhat pleased		extremely pleased
1	2	3	4	5

Leisure Time:

Circle how pleasing your leisure, non- work related activities are with your spouse

| 1 | 2 | 3 | 4 | 5 |

Describe leisure time that is pleasing to you.

_____
_____
_____
_____
_____
_____
_____
_____
_____
_____
_____
_____
_____
_____
_____
_____
_____
_____
_____
_____
_____
_____
_____
_____
_____
_____

Quality Time:

Describe what is quality time to you.

_____

_____

_____

_____

_____

_____

_____

_____

_____

_____

_____

_____

_____

_____

_____

_____

_____

_____

_____

_____

_____

_____

Homebody:

Least important	somewhat important	extremely important
1	2	3	4	5

On the Go:

Least important	somewhat important	extremely important
1	2	3	4	5

List activities that you enjoy the most.

_____
_____
_____
_____
_____
_____
_____
_____
_____
_____
_____
_____
_____

List activities that you enjoy together.

_____
_____
_____
_____
_____
_____
_____
_____
_____
_____
_____
_____
_____

Spiritually:

Are you pleased with the spiritual climate of your relationship?

Least pleased   somewhat pleased   extremely pleased

1   2   3   4   5

Prayer together:

Least pleased   somewhat pleased   extremely pleased

1   2   3   4   5

Worship together:

Least pleased   somewhat pleased   extremely pleased

1   2   3   4   5

Converse about spiritual matters:

Least pleased   somewhat pleased   extremely pleased

1   2   3   4   5

Study the Bible together:

Least pleased   somewhat pleased   extremely pleased

1   2   3   4   5

Share spiritual experiences:

Least pleased   somewhat pleased   extremely pleased

1   2   3   4   5

Now that you have both completed the assessment chose your main ideas. The main ideas are those character traits, passions, and areas of importance in the assessment that are extremely important to you and have a lower level circled for your spouse's performance. Meaning, they are not meeting your expectations and are not pleasing you in that particular area.

Example:

> Mary underlined "compassion" in the personality traits as extremely high and also circled "kids moral values" high as well. Although she circled other things in her script as extremely high, compassion and the kid's moral values were assessed at 2 and 1 respectively. These are her main ideas.
>
> The goal of any director is to work on "chunks" of the script at a time by rehearsing. Although you have much to work on in your scripts, take only 2 – 3 main ideas at a time. Rehearsals take time to perfect. Since none of us are perfect, we can expect times of failure and even our performances may call for a tomato throwing exhibition! So our number one rule at writing our scripts is to choose only 2-3 "main ideas" for your spouse to rehearse. There is room on the next two pages for both you and your spouse to write your Scripts.

HIS "Main Ideas"

HER "Main Ideas"

Endnotes:

Introduction

1. Humpty Dumpty, Public Domain
2. (Augustine) http://en.wikipedia.org/wiki/Augustine_of_Hippo.
3. (Aquinas) http://www.freeessays.cc/db/18/eft6.shtml.
4. (Martin Luther) Peter Vardy, The Puzzle of Sex (M.E. Sharpe 1997) p, 80.
5. The Hebrew word "Checed" can be studied further through the Hebrew spelling "Chesed" http://en.wikipedia.org/wiki/Chesed; another resource is the O.T. Hebrew Lexicon, http://www.studylight.org/lex/heb/view.cgi?number=02617.
6. Ibid (Checed)

"Reconciliation"

7. Willard F. Harley Jr. and Jennifer Harley Chalmers, Surviving An Affair, (Revell, 1998)p,71

"Your Way Right Away"

8. Dictionary.com (Intimacy)

"You've Lost That Lovin' Feelin"

9. The Righteous Brothers. You've Lost That Lovin' Feelin'. Philles 124, 1964, #1

"You Scratch My Back, I'll Scratch Yours"

10. (for "A-res-ko" Greek word) http://www.biblestudytools.net/Lexicons/Greek/grk.cgi?number=700&version=kjv

"All The World's A Stage"

11. Ibid (Aresko)

"Create an Ethos"

12. "Ethos" http://en.wikipedia.org/wiki/Ethos
13. Ibid. (Ethos)

"Conflict Resolution-The Three C's"

14. Donald G. McNeil Jr., "THE NATION; Why So Many More Americans Die in Fire," NYTIMES (DEC. 22, 1991)

Websites:

www.30daysexchallenge.com

www.blog.relevantchurch.com

www.davidclarkeseminars.com

www.marriagebuilders.com